The HUTTERITE

TREASURY of RECIPES

Compiled and edited by: **Sam Hofer**

Book design by: **Sam Hofer**

Illustrations by: **Paul Freitag & Sam Hofer**

Published by

HOFER PUBLISHING
(ON THE PRAIRIE)
719 McPHERSON AVE.
SASKATOON, SK.
S7N 0X9

5th
Edition

To all cooks and lovers of
ethnic cooking...

SAM HOFER

First Printing (First Edition)..............Oct. 1984
Second Printing(Second Edition)...........Oct. 1985
Third Printing ....Dec. 1985
Fourth Printing (Third Edition)............ Apr.1986
Fifth Printing .... May 1986
Sixth Printing .... May 1986
Seventh Printing(Fourth Printing)....... June 1986
Eighth Printing................................... Aug. 1986
Ninth Printing(Fifth Edition)...............Oct. 1986
Tenth Printing .... Nov. 1986
Eleventh Printing ....Dec. 1986
Twelfth Printing................................Feb. 1987

Table of Contents:

LIST YOUR FAVORITES

Recipes	Page

FOREWORD

The fifth edition of the **Hutterite Treasury of Recipes** is a combination of the unbiased history of the Hutterite way of life, and their traditional cooking.

The concept for this book originated while still living in the Hutterite community, where I noticed the tremendous amount of interest and enjoyment outside visitors expressed while touring my home colony. Some of these visitors chancing to get invited into the **Communal Kitchen** for a meal with the whole community, would many times respond by asking the cooks about the unique recipes that were prepared.

It was with great pleasure that I began gathering original Hutterite recipes from various colonies in the country, many never before published.

The **Hutterite Treasury of Recipes** gives you the original taste of the Hutterian Kitchens for your enjoyment at home.

THE TYPICAL HUTTERITE KITCHEN

1. DINING HALL
2. PORCHES
3. DOOR TO CELLAR
4. THE BELL

5. COOKING AREA
6. UNLOADING DOOR
7. REFRIGERATION AREA
8. BAKERY

THE CENTRE OF BAILDON COLONY
NEAR MOOSE JAW, SAKATCHEWAN.

AT TOP PART OF PHOTOGRAPH IS
A GARDEN SIMILAR TO DESCRIPTION   ON PAGE 33.

THE GRAINERIES SIMILAR TO
DESCRIPTION ON PAGE 33.

The History of the Hutterites
(In Europe)

To fully explain the history of the Hutterites, it is neccessary to go back in time as far as when Jesus Christ lived on Earth.

Following Jesus Christ's $3\frac{1}{2}$ years of preaching, resurrection and ascent into Heaven, Christ sent the Holy Spirit from Heaven to enrich the Church of Christ. This time in history is represented by what we call the day of the Pentecost today. This occured 30 A.D.. At that time the deciples of Jesus Christ first established and practiced the communion of all goods, Chapter 2 of Acts. However, it was several centuries later when that way of life was practiced by the Hutterites.

The early Church of Christ spread rapidly as persecution set in against the Christians, to Europe and along the coast of the Mediterrean Sea. From 250 A.D. to 310 A.D. the Christians were persecuted very severely as the Pagan rulers made their governments enforce extreme persecutions on these Christians until 311 A.D., when Christianity was legalized by the Roman Emperor, Constantine.

Due to conflict with the Catholic Church, the Protestant Church was born on October 31, 1517, when Martin Luther voiced his opinion by nailing 95 thesis on the church door at Wittenburg, Germany, in his objections to the Catholic Church. Luther and his followers formed a separate church which is well known today as the Lutheran Church.

Two leaders from Switzerland, Calvin and Zwingli who, like Luther, had also broken away from the Catholic Church established what we now know is the Reformed and Presbyterian churches. These leaders respectively insisted that people must belong to the ruling church and must have their babies baptized into the new church.

However, some of the men who worked with Zwingli were disatisfied and felt the need for a free voluntary church. Because they could not recognize infant baptism, they began re-baptizing each other, therefore calling themselves anabaptists (re-baptizers).

The code of their beliefs were as follows:
° Baptism upon confession of faith, rather then being baptized when only an infant.
° Belief in the way of love, instead of war, strife and violence.
° Opposition to the oath and swearing.
° Belief in separation from the world.

Some of these early leaders of the anabaptist movement were Menno Simon, Balthaser Hubmaier and Jacob Hutter. Many of these early leaders were highly educated, intelligent men many of whom were ex-monks or Hebrew scholars. Later these 3 leaders mentioned above were to play the chief roles of establishing the Mennonite and Hutterite groups.

Persecution set in immediately, directed against these leaders. Disagreeing with the anabaptists, Calvin, Zwingli and Luther, as were as other "State" churches joined forces with the Catholics in an attempt to kill the movement.

This persecution drove many of the anabaptist preachers from Switzerland to South Germany and Austria.

In July, 1526 at Nikolsburg, Moravia, Dr. Bathaser Hubmaier organized a church of over 6000 members. These members come from all over Switzerland, South Germany, the Tyrol, Schleswig and upper Austria to escape persecution. From this large group of anabaptists were to come the Mennonites, Hutterites, Amish, Prairieleut, etc..

At this time the Turks were threatening war on Moravia. When the government asked the people of Moravia to bear arms, some of the members of this Anabaptist Church believed that under no circumstances can a true follower and believer in Christ bear arms. They believed that the perfect way to live, was to have all things in common as practiced in Chapter 2 of Acts, as mentioned earlier. The leader of this group, Jacob Wiedeman, left Nikolsburg in 1528 with his group and travelled to Austerlitz, seeking refuge.

They stopped at Bogenitz on their way, and spread a cloth on the ground and all members placed their material possesions on it. This was the beginning of a way of life which is still practiced amongst the Hutterites of South Dakota, Montana, and the Prairie Provinces of Canada.

Jacob Wiedeman, lacking leadership, appealed to Jacob Hutter, who was also a believer in Community way of life. Because Jacob Hutter was a good organizer and practiced strict discipline, he became the leader of this congregation. Therefore, these people were called Hutterites.

Going back over the early history of the Hutterites, it is found that the Hutterites were under almost continuous persecution. Whatever wealth and peace they established for themselves in years between heavy persecution was all plundered and destroyed by their persecutors. For a small group of people who have been and are so set in their beliefs against war, they have probably been subject to its consequences more than any other group. Wherever they fled to, they were always, within a few years, either chased out, murdered or sold to slavery by their plunderers and persecutors. Because they wouldn't fight back, they were very easy prey indeed, and all they ever wanted was peace, and to be left alone.

Between 1550 - 1564, a period of heavy persecution, its reported in the Hutterite Chronicles that 16 Colonies were destroyed. During these times some 81 members were murdered and 140 sold to slavery to Turkey. Following this persecution, there were some good years. During the reign of Maximillian 2, Between 1564 - 1576 and a number of years after his reign, the Hutterites grew in numbers. They established about 86 Hutterite Brunderhofs (Colonies) in Moravia and Hungary. Each Colony had between 3 to 4 hundred people. Similar to Hutterites today, the Colonies then were mostly of agricultural, large heads of cattle and fine breeds of horses. In these days they also manufatured cutlery and pottery, which were sold and all revenue put together into the Treasury.

Following the good years, a religious war broke out in 1618. This war lasted till 1648. As a result of this war, many armies marched through the country, plundering down Hutterite Colonies, robbing their good and killing many Hutterite men.

To make matters worse, the Austrian government issued a decree in September of 1622 stating that any Hutterite still left in Moravia after 4 weeks would be put to death. The persecuted Hutterites fled, leaving behind 24 bruderhofs, filled with grains, cattle, horses, oxen, hogs and goods of all kinds. They fled over the Hungarian Mountains to seek refuge amongst their Mennonite brethern in Hungary. There they established 3 large Bruderheims; Sabotisch, Brotska and Lewar. The smallest of the three had a population of over 3000 people.

Following the 30 years religious war, the Turkish wars began. These wars almost wiped out the Hutterites completely. In 1686, the Hutterites decided to abandon their community way of life. It seemed foolish to have their large supplies of food in one place, only to have the Turks raid them repeatedly, leaving them with nothing for their hard work.

During the 18th Century, survival was terribly hard for the Hutterites. When in 1760 the Jesuits recieved permission from Maria Theresa to force Hutterites to convert to Catholism, Hutterite ministers were imprisoned and promised freedom only if they accepted the other faith. Many of them accepted that offer, being tired of the persecution.

As a result of many of the Hutterites converting to Catholism and the repeated raids by the Turks, they were reduced to poverty. To help each other out they switched back and forth between community life and private ownership several times; the Hutterite Chronicles report that by the early 1760's, heavy persecution had reduced the number of Hutterites practicing the communal life to a mere handful.

Throughout this persecution, two of these remaining people, banished from the country because there was no way possible that anyone could convert them into another faith, wandered into Romania. There they found prosperous people who were giving religious freedom. They returned to inform their brethern about their new place to live, and along with a large number of Lutheran exiles from Carinthia, who had accepted the Hutterian way of life, fled Maria Theresa's empire. They crossed the Carpathian mountains into Romania. There they established a Bruderhof colony near Bucharest.

Their peace was short lived. Only a year later, in 1767 the Turks swept down on them once again when war broke out between Turkey and Russia.Fortunately, through a Russian general, camping near their Colony, they were informed that they would be welcome in Russia. Cazarina, Catherine the Great of Russia was encouraging and welcoming German farmers to her country to improve lands that needed developing. The Hutterites, bewildered by all these moves, yet knowing that they had to get out of Romania, accepted the move as God's will and after prayerful consideration, the group of 123 decided to head for Russia.

The General was very helpful by giving them a pair of oxen and a wagon to continue their journey, as well as the proper credentials to pass into Russia. It was arranged by the Field Marshal Romanzof, whose land they would be farming and with whom they made their contracts with, that they were given the guidance and protection to cross Poland and safely into Russia. There they were advanced immediate necessities such as food, housing and barns for their cattle. In addition, money, lumber for homes, land and hay was also advanced to them. All this was granted to them with a three year exemption period, after which they would pay a definite price.

In Russia, the Hutterites were granted freedom of religion and their own self government. Because of their reputation of being good farmers, hard workers and if being very industrious, they were given the opportunity to continue their lifestyle without hindrance, as drawn up in the contract made with the Russians.

They settled down at Wischinka by the Desna River, where they immediately started building their barns and homes.

By the middle of 1771, the Hutterites had a new Bruderhof built on their own property. With farming and industries such as pottery, weaving and metals, the Bruderhofs soon became very wealthy.

For the next 100 years the Hutterites lived in Russia. Even though their haven in Russia was rather short lived, as they still had various tribulations and problems over the years, they still managed to do pretty well for themselves.

It was 1874 when the Russian government started the conscription law. The Hutterites were given two choices. They could stay and serve the Russian Army or they had to leave Russia. They decided to leave the country.

* * * * * * * *

THE HISTORY OF THE HUTTERITES IN EUROPE IS BASED ON REFERENCES FROM WITHIN THE HISTORY OF THE HUTTERITE MENNONITES 1974 BY PINE HILL PRESS. FREEMAN, S. DAKOTA.

(In North America)

With the Russian government threatening to pass the conscription law in 1872, several groups, some of which were the Hutterites and Mennonites, gave careful consideration to countries like Australia, South America and North America as countries which to migrate to.

Many favorable reports of North America brought back by various groups and individuals added considerable impetus to the immigration movement. It was decided that a delegation would be sent out from various groups of people to investigate the promised land more fully and to report its findings to the respective villages.

A delegation of 12 men, some of which were Hutterites, was assigned this journey to America.

They set sail in April of 1873 and landed at New York after an ocean trip of 13 days. Here the delegation split up and went in different directions. The Hutterites toured Indiana, they travelled to Chicago, Illinois and on to St. Paul, Minnesota. They also toured parts of the Dakotas, Nebraska and Kansas, as well as parts of Manitoba. It was found that the frontier of America where cheap lands and free lands were still available in quantities for large settlements run from Winnipeg, south through the Red River Valley, across the southeastern corner of Dakota, through central Nebraska and Kansas, down into Texas. Their recommendation upon returning to Russia was to migrate to America and settle somewhere in these territories.

Thus, provisions for moving to America began and neccessary passports were obtained, permitting emigration tion from Russia. This however, wasn't an overnight task, because there were many thousands of people from other groups including the German Lutherans, Reformed and Catholics trying to emigrate from Russia. The Russian government, realizing that a mass migration was underway and that there was a good possibility that Russia would lose some 40,000 of its most industrious farmers in south Russia, made efforts to stem the tide. As a result, some of the Hutterites as well as other groups did not leave Russia, and later suffered the many hardships of the revolution that followed.

However, most of the Hutterites did manage to emigrate from Russia and settle in America. A group of 250 Shmiedleut and Dariusleut Hutterites as well as other groups such as the low Germans and Swiss from Russian Poland, set sail from Hamburg on the 'Harmonia' and landed in New York on July 17, 1874. The Hutterites travelled to Detroit and then to Chicago, through Nebraska, and finally into the Dakotas, where they found a suitable tract of land on which the first group, the Shmiedleut Hutterites settled. The Shmiedleut (Blacksmith people) were led by Michael Waldner, who was a blacksmith. This first colony was established in Bon Homme County, located on the Missouri River, some 18 miles from Yankton. This original Shmiedleut Colony was named Bon Homme Colony. The second of the three original

Communal Hutterites were the Dariusleut Hutterites, named after their leader Darius Walter, settled temperarily near Silver Lake and a year later in 1875, settled permanently at Wolf Creek, forty miles north of Bon Homme, near the James River. The third group, called the Lehreleut Hutterites, teacher's people, after their leader, Jacob Wipf, who was a teacher, came to America a bit later in 1877. They settled near Parkston. This colony was called the Elmspring Colony.

It is estimated that between 1874 and 1879, some 1200 Hutterites emigrated from Russia. Two thirds of these Hutterites were non-communal Hutterites. These people were called Prairieleut. The Prairieleut shared the same language, religion and ancestry with the communal Hutterites, and in the early years in America, the communal Hutterites and the Prairieleut were very close. Marriages between colony and non-colony members took place, some joining the colonies, while others left the colonies. Later, because of differences in lifestyles and organizations they began growing apart. Many of the Prairieleut later joined the Mennonite Brethren and the General Conference Mennonites.

The three original Hutterite communites spread out into seventeen communities in South Dakota during the 40 years following their coming to America. During this time two colonies were also established in Montana. The first one was established at Lewistown in 1912. During these 40 years the Hutterites experienced the freedom to follow their lifestyle without hindrance.

However, in 1914, with the coming of World War I once again they were subject to conflict. Because of their refusal to buy Liberty Bonds and because of their refusal to take part in the war, the Hutterites were resented severely and acts of violence and theft were commited against them. Some of the young men who were drafted for military service and taken to the army camps, upon refusal to put on uniforms, were severely starved and beaten. At Alcatraz some members were tortured with enough severity to cause their death. This shook up the Hutterites very badly and as the resentment against them got worse, they saw no other alternative but to immigrate to another country. Because they had formerly considered Canada and were welcomed to that country by the government, they decided to move there. Religious freedom was promised to them in Canada.

Almost immediately, in 1918, all the Hutterite settlements in South Dakota, except one, began their move. The Schmiedleut settled in Manitoba; the Dariusleut and Lehreleut in Alberta. However, in a few years, during the 1930's, because of changes in legislation in the Dakotas, some of the Schmiedleut from Manitoba once again inhabited their former colonies in South Dakota. The Dariusleut and the Lehreleut colonies, which still owned land in South Dakota, sold out to the Schmiedleut. Today, all colonies in South Dakota and Manitoba are Schmiedleut Hutterites. The Dariusleut and Lehreleut Hutterites have branched out in Alberta, Saskatchewan and Montana.

The first colony in Saskatchewan was established at Shaunavon in 1914. Over the years, there have been over three hundred colonies established throughout the northwestern United States and southwestern Canada, most of which are situated in the three prairie provinces of Canada and South Dakota and Montana in the United States. Only a few colonies have been established in North Dakota, Minnesota and Washington.

The Hutterites have continued their industry as mixed farmers, because the farming lifestyle fits their particular way of life best.

This in a nutshell is the basic history of the Hutterites, when and how they first started in Europe, their migration to North America and their growth in this country.

* * * * * * * *

THE DINING HALL

A tour through a Hutterite Colony.

The typical Hutterite colony looks like a large farmyard, complete with barns, machinery, shops and garages. On the other hand it also looks liks a small village, complete with houses, a church house, unnamed streets, lawns, trees, a garden and people. And that is exactly what a Hutterite Colony is; a small farm village. This village is complete with all the facilities to be practically self-sufficient, to the effect that it has many skilled people for running various operations like hog farming, dairy farming, poultry farming, grain farming, mechanical works, gardening, construction, shoe making, tailoring, crafts, baking, cooking and much more. For an outsider to visit a Hutterite Colony, this can be a very interesting experience. It could be compared to stepping into a different country, because the Hutterites have maintained alot of their European origin, with the way they dress and the way they conduct themselves. The reason for maintaining the dressing is because their dress and their appearance takes on a theological significance and is a mark of their distinctiveness from the world. This also, internally unites the community and discourages vanity and an interest in worldly fashions.

The whole colony is built upon what their way of life means and examplifies; the way of Communal living; in other words, keeping all things in common.

Although I left the Hutterite way of life a few years ago, after spending the first 21 years of my life in the colony, the Hutterite lifestyle and growing up in such an environment, means alot to me, as it normally would and should. Part of my upbringing has instilled in me strict dicipline in conducting myself in pursuits of my goals, which the Hutterite lifestyle advocates in its own cause.

A short while ago, I had the privelege and delightful opportunity of touring one of the many Hutterite Colonies in the country with some friends from the city. We arrived at the Colony shortly after 2:00 in the after- noon. As we parked our car, we were greeted by several young girls, who in obvious excitement, offered them- selves as our tour guides. Even though I could have found my way around easily, I still appreciated the girls' offer.

Since we had parked in the center of the Colony, our first step on our tour was the kitchen. I explained to my friends, that the kitchen is a gathering place for the whole community. Here, people gather for breakfast, dinner, supper, coffee breaks and various other activities. I explained that it is now customary for Hutterites to build their kitchen and their church house together into one big long building, devided only by a sound proof wall. I briefly pointed out that these two buildings, the kitchen and the church house, are the most important edifices in the Hutterite society. It is here that everybody in the Colony comes together for both physical and spiritual nourishment.

Inside the kitchen the lingering smell of roasted cabbage greeted us. Responding, I remembered how I used to love the roasted cabbage. I explained to my friends that roasted cabbage is almost always eaten on Wednesdays and Sundays for dinner along with stewed duck or hens. There was only one woman in the kitchen at this time. She invited us in, curious of who my guests were, whom I briefly introduced. As the head cook, she was already planning supper for 6:30. As soon as her two helpers would arrive at 4:00, they would start setting the tables, followed shortly by preparing the eggs, milk and flour. I guessed it. Some 115 people would be eating Russian pancakes for supper this evening. I explained to my friends that all the women are devided into pairs and each pair is given one week in the bakery, followed by one week in the kitchen helping the head cook.

Asking the head cook to show my curious friends the stewing vats used for soups, stewing meats, pickling or frying, she proudly showed us the large homemade stainless steel vats, explaining that she's capable of stewing or frying up to 30 chickens at one time, enough to feed the whole colony.

Inside the bakery, we briefly looked at the large dough mixer, capable of mixing up to 200 lbs. of flour at one time and the large oven in which as many as 50 loaves of bread can be baked at one time.

After touring the bakery, we were led into the large and spacious dining hall termed as the Ess Stum. Pointing to the left, I explained that, like in the church house, during the meal, all men are seated to one side, according to age. The women are also seated according to age, on the opposite side. Everybody is seated in fours, with younger men closest to the door. This enables the youngest member of the Leut, people older than 14 years of age, to fetch whatever is needed; missing silverware, plates, cups and to tell the cooks about any serving that may need replenishing. The youngest girl will also fetch whatever is needed for the women. One of the older men is given the job of bread-cutting. When bread is needed, a sharp rap on the table with a spoon, signals that bread is needed in the area of the rap. After everybody is settled in his or her respective place, the farm boss, when present, will signal everyone to become quiet by saying, 'Vir Ven Beten, (we will pray)' and with everybody folding his or her hands like in prayer; he recites his short verse of prayer. After saying grace, the youngest girls will serve the food, in servings of four, because all men and women are devided in fours, ensuring the even distribution of the food. At the end of the meal the field boss signals everybody to become quiet again by saying, 'Vir Ven Danken, (we will say our thanks.)' Fifteen minutes later, the children 6 to 13 years of age will take their turns at the table.

We walked from the kitchen, eager to see the rest of the colony.

Looking about, I couldn't help but notice that this particular colony was almost alike in general layout as the colony I had grown up in. The long apartment like houses were the same length and width as back home.

The girls led us inside one of the houses, and showed us the interior. My friends were somewhat surprised by the simplicity of this home. The apartment that was shown to us consisted of a living room, 2 bedrooms and a washroom. The first room, which was the living room, was furnished with a table, straight chairs, and a cupboard. The bedrooms were furnished very simply with 2 double beds, a chest of drawers and a wooden chest. Each family, according to size is given 1 to 3 apartments to live in.

In response to one of my friends asking whether or not Hutterites have television or radio in their homes, I told her that TV and radio are strictly forbidden in the Hutterite community, adding that one time while still in the colony at home, the younger men had sneaked a TV set into the dairy barn to watch some hockey games. Shortly after, it was detected and destroyed by the preacher, who didn't want us to learn more about the outside world than absolutely neccessary. The whole purpose of the sheltered life in the colony is to abstain from worldly activities by simply not becoming a part of them, even to the extent of ignoring their existence.

Completing the tour of the house, we stopped to converse with a lady in her late forties. As we learned, she was busy designing a wedding dress for her daughter, who was getting married in 3 weeks. She explained that the wedding dress is basically the same style as a normal Hutterite dress, although the wedding dress would be cut more decorative, using highly resplendent colors. Another, younger woman, the bride-to-be, was busy sewing together what she explained were brand new pants and jackets for her 3 brothers, to be worn at this special event. When we asked her how she had first met her boyfriend, she told us that 2 years before while at another colony, helping with the interior decorating of a house being remodeled, the two of them had met and fell in love. Ever since then, her boyfriend had come every 6 weeks to see her.

I briefly explained the basic wedding traditions in a Hutterite colony to my touring companions. The perspective groom accompanied by his father and other close relatives, begin by making a trip to the girl's colony, seeking permission from her and the consent of the colony. Following the affirmative response of the girl and her parents, a special engagement service is held in the church house. This is followed by an evening stübela (festivity) in the communal kitchen, where the whole community enjoys refreshments and singing of wedding songs. This festivity is continued, sometimes till midnight. The festivity is repeated 2 weeks following the first one, once again on the girl's colony. The next day, the suitor departs to his own colony, taking with him his bride-to-be, her immediate family and her belongings. On this colony, another Stübela (festivity), takes place in the evening. The couple is wed following the Sunday morning sermon. The marriage ceremony is followed by a wedding meal, served with beer, wine, and soft drinks and attended by the whole community. The whole afternoon is enjoyed by singing melodious and very cheerful German songs and wedding songs while snacks are served and drinks are replenished. In the evening, after visiting with relatives and guests, the couple goes to their newly prepared apartment.

While explaining the Hutterite wedding traditions, we had slowly moved onward and were now at our next stop, the slaughter house. Here we were shown all the homemade equipment used for this type of work, as well as several large 50 gallon vats used for canning and pickling during the summer months. The girls showed us a homemade pea shelling machine run by a small electric motor, designed to shell up to 10 lbs. of peas per minute. Outside the building, we were shown some 25, huge, 10 foot long burlap bags, stuffed with duck feathers, removed from the batch of ducks slaughtered the day before. These feathers, when dry would be stuffed into large bags and shipped to a wholesaler later on in the fall. Some will be used to make pillows and quilts with, many of which would be sold by the colony.

The next stops on our tour were the barns. Noting

the size of the buildings and the large numbers of
animals that were raised here, we were very impressed.
I asked the overseer in the dairy department on the size
of his herd to which he laughingly replied, "only 80 cows
now, but we're expanding to double this size next spring."

Due to regulations, we didn't get to walk into the
hog barn. However, we did get to chat with the Herdsman, who seemed very glad to get the opportunity to
tell about his centre of influence, consisting of a farrow
to finish 400 sow operation, all built into 3, joined
together, two hundred and thirty foot long barns, with
a large fifty foot high leg elevator used to distribute
several tons of feed each day, directly from its very
own highly computerized feed manufacturing plant. He
too, like the Dairy Herdsman, commented by saying that
even though with his hands full at the present time, he
still would like to upgrade his facilities and build an
even larger hog operation. He explained that the hog
operation is one of the colony's chief assets.

Stopping to watch a flock of geese out on a field
of grass in the duck and goose area of the colony, I
was momentarily taken back in memory to my home
colony, where together with my parents and one of
my brothers, used to hatch up to 2000 little goslings
each spring, as well as purchase and raise the usual
flock of over 1200 ducks. Most of these birds were sold,
fully dressed, ready for cooking, to customers in neighbor-
ing towns and villiages, either door to door or our regular
customers would come to the colony for their usual
number.

Our next stop were the chicken barns. We stepped into
the laying hen barn, impressed by the number of egg
cases stacked neatly in one large walk-in refrigerator.
Although the chicken overseer was obviously very busy
grading eggs, he did stop for a moment to talk with us.
I asked him how many eggs his flock produces, to which
he replied, that once a week his wholesale customer
picks up approximately 4500 dozens of eggs, and he
himself grades and delivers up to 800 dozens to his
retail customers in the city every week. He also mentioned that he raises up to 30,000 broilers each year,
most of which are sold fully dressed, ready for cooking,
to regular and waiting customers.

The colony's next attraction was its 20 acre garden. Surrounded by miles of Elm trees in rows
between various sections for wind protection, the garden had the appearance of a small forest. We stopped
to count the $\frac{1}{4}$ mile long rows of corn, cabbage, and
carrots, but lost count after 250. We found the gardener
in the orchard where, with the help of several young
women, he was busy loading crab-apples unto a trailer,
which the women had been picking all afternoon. I
queried the group as to what they were to do with the
crab-apples. The gardener explained that most of the
apples would be used for making apple juice, while the
rest would be canned for consumption over the winter.

We briefly stopped to photograph three 160 feet
feet long graineries and a whole mass of metal bins
used for grain storage. Judging from the size of the

bins and graineries, I estimated that the capacity
combined here, must be well over 200,000 bushels of
grain when full. While the number of acreage each colony
has may vary, some colonies have up to 8,000 acres on
which mostly wheat, barley, and hay crops are produced.
Some other crops produced are flax, rye field, peas,
rapeseed and sugar beets.

As our tour of the colony continued, we were shown
into a carpentry shop, a blacksmith shop, and garages.
In the carpentry shop, a short but heavy set man, proudly
demonstrated his equipment for us. He pointed out that
as the carpenter assigned by the colony, he was respon-
sible for building whatever furniture was required by
the colony such as, tables, benches, chairs, chest of
drawers, cupboards, shelves and alot more. He is also
the overseer in any construction which involves lumber
and concrete. His older brother, both the electrician and
plumber, has been assigned by the colony to oversee
these departments while another brother is assigned to
the whole fleet of motor vehicles, including 3 large
tandem trucks, 2 smaller two-ton trucks, 2 vans, 2 super-
cab pick-up trucks, and one large bus as well as 3 other
half ton trucks that the colony uses for odd jobs on
the field or on the colony grounds.

On our next stop, we didn't get to talk to anyone.
A person who the girls pointed out to be the blacksmith,
was obviously very busy welding together, what I
guessed to be a feed bin. He was inside the bin with
his arc welder, electronically gluing the seams together.

The blacksmith of the colony has yet another very
important job. Besides building various machines and
appliances used in shops and throughout the whole
colony, he is almost always there for repair jobs when
machines like the rock picker, cultivators, trailers, trucks
or tractors requiring his special skill of welding.

Our next stop was the tractor garage. I recalled
that back home in the colony, as young men, each of us
were assigned one or two tractors to maintain, repair
when needed, and operate, along with whatever machinery
assigned to each one's particular tractor. I remembered
the first tractor assigned to me by the farm boss. My
brother and cousin had left the colony to try the outside
world for a while. I being next in line according to age,
was assigned to maintain and operate an 830 Case tractor.
Along with my new promotion was included the job of
maintaining and operating several machines like the rock
picker, the manure spreader, and small mower, the portable feed mill as well as hauling water to the fields
when spraying the crops with insecticides and
herbicides.   Later, on top of all the above, I was
also assigned by the field boss to maintain and
operate the back hoe tractor.

On the first major repair job, it was required to
replace a warn clutch, which with the help of an older
and more experienced member of the colony, just simply
following the instructions outlined in the manual and by
using common sense, we replaced it within a day and a
half. What I was saying is that in the colony, like on

most farms, one doesn't learn by years of studies to become skilled at something, one simply takes on most tasks, regardless how difficult, till its complete. When help is needed, someone with more experience is asked for directions.

In the garage, 2 young men were busy replacing the fuel injection system of a large 4 wheel drive tractor. I started speaking in the Hutterite Slavic German dialect to them, asking them what they were doing. They responded at once, looking at me wide eyed, and asked me in the same Slavic German dialect, " from which colony are you from?". After exchanging introductions, the men decided to take a short break and joined us on the way to the car, somewhat thrilled at meeting an ex-Hutterite from another colony. They explained that one of their brothers and a cousin had left the colony a year ago, but were contemplating on returning the following spring. I pointed out to my friends from the city, that even though quite a few people do leave the colony, most of which are young men, a lot of these people do eventually go back to live in the colony. One's upbringing in the colony, combined with the religious training, is instilled in most people as the perfect way to spend one's life. Communal life, separated from the outside world and its many complications, is considered and taught as the way that God wishes them to live. The colony has always eagerly welcomed back their own people, even after many years of departure from the colony. A person is welcomed back under the condition that he once again follow the colony's lifestyle like before.

We left the Hutterite Colony at about 5:30, just shortly before the daily church service.

If you are interested in touring a Hutterite colony, simply phone the colony neares to you or any colony of your choice and inform them that you would like to tour their community. They will let you know what time is best. For continued reading on the Hutterites, the following books are recommended.

HUTTERITE SOCIETY BY John A. Hostetler.

THE HUTTERITES (A Study in Prejudice) by David Flint.

THE HUTTERITES IN NORTH AMERICA by John A. Hostetler.

THE HUTTERITE WAY by Paul S. Gross

These books are available in many book stores and libraries in North America.

Soups, Borschts, Salads, & Sauces

BUCKWHEAT GRITZ

10 cups chicken or duck broth
1 cup buckwheat
4 eggs

Bring the broth to a boil and add the well-mixed and slightly beaten eggs and buckwheat. Boil for 25 minutes, not vigorously. Salt to taste.

HOMEMADE SOUP

5 bouillon cubes
½ small head cabbage
1 bunch carrots
2 stalks celery
½ green pepper

1 can green beans
1 can tomatoes
1 can tomato sauce
5 cups water

Cook all ingredients over medium heat till carrots are tender. Salt to taste. Add additional spices, if you prefer.

TREPHLICH
(Egg Drops)

1 bowl milk   2 eggs

Slightly beat the eggs. Bring the milk to a boil, in a double boiler, and combine the eggs and let boil slightly till the eggs sre thick and lumpy. Sweeten with honey or brown sugar. A simple and nutritious recipe.

HUTTERITE BORSCHT

4 cups chicken, duck or beef broth	1 cup cream
2 cups cabbage (shredded)	1 tbsp. flour
½ cup sliced carrots	1 tbsp. sugar

Cook the cabbage and carrots in the broth (not vigorously) for five minutes or until tender. Beat the cream, flour and sugar together and combine with the vegetables and broth. Cook for another five minutes on medium heat.

CARROT SOUP

3 cups carrots (shredded)	3 cups milk
3/4 cup fine chopped onions	1 cup shredded cheese
2 tbsp. flour	salt, pepper and sugar
2 tbsp. butter	to taste

Cook carrots in boiling water with soup base for 10 minutes. Melt butter; saute onions until soft, about 5 minutes. Stir in flour, seasoning and sugar. Gradually add milk and cook. Add carrots and liquid. Add cheese and stir until melted. Let cheese melt in milk and pour into soup.

POTATO SOUP

Cook the bone of a ham (with some meat on it) in 1½ quarts of water. Add 4 large potatoes peeled and cut in little pieces. Add one small onion, (not cut up at all). Cook this until potatoes are soft. Mix 1 tbsp. flour with ½ cup cream and add to the soup.

To keep vegetables green while cooking, lift lid from vessel from time to time.

CREAM OF VEGETABLE SOUP

5 cups water
3/4 cup corn
1½ cups carrots (sliced)
3/4 cup pea pods
1¼ tsp. salt

1¼ cups ½ inch potato cubes
1 ¼ tbsp. chicken soup base
1 tsp. sugar
1/3 cup cream

Combine all ingreadients; the cream last of all. Mix well and cook for 10 to 15 minutes or until vegetables are tender. Stir while cooking. Add a small amount of flour while cooking.

BORSCHT NO.1

Cook hock of pork in 1½ quarts of water to make soup. Take soup and add 1 small head cabbage, cut up; 1 large beet, cut in small pieces; 1 medium onion, sliced; 1 cup peas; 1 cup carrots; 1 cup corn; 1 pint tomatoes. Add 1 tbsp. sugar. Just before serving, add ½ cup cream.

BORSCHT NO. 2 (Large Recipe)

Cook 2 pounds beef in 1½ quarts of water until almost done. Season with salt, pepper and garlic salt. Add:

1 small head cabbage, shredded
1 can beans
1 can peas
sliced carrots

3 potatoes, cubed
1 small onion
1 pint tomatoes

Simmer. Just before serving add ½ cup cream. Heat to boiling point. Serve.

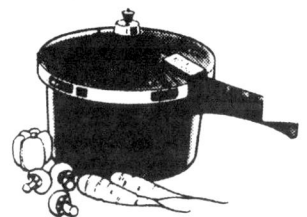

To restore freshness in frozen vegetables, pour boiling water over them.

KASHA....HUTTERITE POTATO SOUP

4 cups ½ inch potato cubes   5 cups broth that has been
2 tbsp. onion (minced)   used to simmer sausages

This type of potato soup is usually eaten on Saturdays along with pork sausages and sour kraut. Combine all ingredients and cook over medium heat till the potato cubes are tender. Add salt to taste, if desired.

CHICKEN DUMPLINGS

1¼ cup butter or margarine   ½ tbsp. baking powder
7 eggs   1 tbsp. salt
3½ cups flour

Beat butter and egg yolks till creamy. Add to dry ingredients. Stir lightly.

Beat egg whites until stiff. Mix well with the rest of ingredients. Drop into chicken soup broth and cook for 15 minutes. Serve with stewed chicken.

For dessert, prepare gooseberry pudding.

SPAGHETTI SQUASH SOUP

1 quart cooked spaghetti squash   salt to taste
1 small onion   11 cups milk
3 tbsp. chicken soup base   2 tsp. beef base
a dash of pepper   1/3 cup butter

Cook 1 small size squash in its skin. When tender, remove from water and cool. Scoop out insides; discard seeds; wash and drain well. Slice onion and fry in the butter until tender. Heat milk: add squash, onion, the soup bases and then the pepper and salt. Simmer for a few minutes. Serve.

In many colonies KASHA is eaten only in winter and spring months, while the pork sausages are in season.

VEGETABLES WITH DUMPLINGS

½ pound butter   1 3/4 cups carrots
½ quart eggs, beaten   1 3/4 cups celery
5½ cups flour   1 3/4 cups potatoes (cut fine)

Beat butter until creamy: add eggs and flour. Before
adding flour mix a pinch of baking powder with it. This
is your dumpling dough. Cook carrots, celery and potatoes
in broth. The amount of broth you use will determine the
thickness of your mixture after all the vegetables are
added. Don't make the dumplings until the vegetables are
boiled soft and the soup is still cooking. Cook the
dumplings about 10 minutes. Keep checking to see if they
are done.

GASHTEL

7 medium eggs   4 cups flour

Beat the eggs and mix the flour bit by bit while
kneading the dough. Hutterites have a machine that rips
the dough into crumbs the size of grape nuts to pea pods.
When a ripper isn't available, roll the dough out an
1/8 inch thick and let dry real crisp and crumble by hand.
Duck is the usual meat eaten with this type of soup.
Cook the crumbs in the duck broth for 3 minutes before
serving. Salt to taste. Cook 1 cup of crumbs with
2½ cups of duck broth. Season to taste with onion powder.

In many colonies , GASHTEL is eaten
on wednesdays or sundays for dinner.
Roasted cabbage is served with this
meal.

MILCH GASHTEL

Using the Gashtel as described in the recipe above:
Use milk instead of duck broth. Omit the spices.
Simmer the Gashtel in the milk until tender.

CREAMY CARROT SOUP

3 cups carrot (chopped)
2 medium onions
2 cups water
6 tbsp. margerine

1/3 cup flour
1 tsp. salt
soup base to taste
5 cups milk (heated)
parsley (chopped fine)

Cook carrots and onions in the water till tender. Blend.
Melt the margerine, stir in flour and salt. Add milk,
followed by the blended carrots and onions. Add soup
base and let simmer for 5-10 minutes. When serving,
top with parsely.

HUTTERITE NOODLES

6 medium eggs   4 cups flour

Beat the eggs first and combine them with the flour
and knead them into a stiff dough. If a noodle cutting
machine is available, roll the dough out in strips 1/8
to ¼ inch thick, and 6 inches wide before cutting. When
cutting by hand, roll the dough out 1/16 inch and cut
while still wet. The noodles, when cut real fine with
a machine, don't have to be boiled. Simply bring the
broth to a boil and add the noodles before serving.
Serve with stewed chicken or duck, along with roasted
sour cabbage or gooseberry pudding. Like the Gashtel,
you can also cook the noodles in milk.

CREAM OF BEAN SOUP

5 cups chicken broth
2½ cups cut up yellow
string beans
1 cup potatoes (diced)

2½ cups cream
2 tsp. white flour

Cook beans with broth till tender. Add pre-cooked potatoes. Stir flour into cream and stir till smooth. Combine cream with beans and potatoes. Let simmer 2-3 minutes and serve. (Add more cream if you like).

MILK'N BREAD CRUMBS

Heat bowl of milk: soak two or more slices of bread, sweeten with sugar or honey. . . . .
A simple but nutritious helping.

RUSSIAN BORSCHT

4 cups raw potatoes, diced
2 cups cooked navy beans
1 cup pickled beets with juice

salt to taste
½ cup sour cream

Cook potatoes in salted water until tender. Add beans and beets. Bring to a boil. Add sour cream and serve. If you use two medium size beets, raw, add 1 tsp. vinegar and 1 tbsp. sugar. You can add a ham bone to the beans while cooking.

RICE IN MILK

Cook 3/4 cup rice in water till tender. Drain. Add to 1 quart of heated milk. Add ¼ cup raisins before serving. Sweeten with sugar.

NOOK A LA SOUP
(Dumplings)

½ cup butter   ½ tsp. salt
2 large eggs

Use enough flour to make a soft dough that can be
mixed with a spoon. Drop rounded tsps. of dough into
boiling broth, either chicken or beef. Cook for about
5-10 minutes depending on the size of the nook a la.
When making nook a la soup one can figure about one
egg per person.

TOMATO SOUP (Large Recipe)

4 quarts tomatoes   2 onions
4 quarts tomato juice   2 beets
4 carrots

Cook the above ingredients until tender and put through
a blender. Add 1 cup butter, 2 tbsp. soda, 1 tbsp. salt,
1 cup brown sugar. Add 1 gallon of cream milk and
stir while heating. Serve.

HUTTERITE CHILI

1 pound hamburger meat   1½ tsp. chili powder
2 cups kidney beans   3 cups tomatoes
1½ cup onions (chopped fine)

Cook beans until soft. Add all other ingredients. Add
salt to taste. Let simmer until everything is well blended.

TOMATO DRESSING

1/3 cup tomato puree   1 tsp. flour (browned)
1/3 cup lemon juice   ½ cup corn oil
1 medium onion   ½ clove garlic
1 tbsp. honey   1 tsp. salt

Put all ingredients into blender and blend till smooth.
Makes about 1½ cups.

RUSSIAN SALAD DRESSING

1 cup tomatoes or thick juice
½ cup oil (you use whatever oil)
½ cup lemon juice
1 small green onion
1 tbsp. honey

2 tsp. salt
1 tsp. paprika
1 tsp. horseradish
powder (if you wish)
1 garlic bud (if you wish)

Put all the ingredients into food processor. Blend till smooth. Makes about 16 fl. oz.

GOODNESS SALAD DRESSING

1 cup oil
1/3 cup honey
1 tsp. lemon juice
1 tsp. celery seed

1 tsp. paprika
1 tsp. salt
4 tsp. vinegar

Combine all ingredients and use desired amount on shredded cabbage.

COLE SLAW

1 medium head cabbage (shredded)
1 carrot (grated)
1 small onion (cut fine)
¼ cup vinegar

½ cup sugar
½ tsp. salt
½ tbsp. celery seed

Mix vegetables, bring vinegar, sugar, salt and celery seed to a boil. Pour over vegetables while hot. Cool before serving.

If SOUR KRAUT is too sour for your taste, pour hot water over it and drain.

VINEGAR SALAD

Cut enough leafy lettuce from garden for a meal.
Put in desired amount of green onions, add bacon bits
to your taste. For dressing combine $\frac{1}{4}$ cup vinegar to
$\frac{1}{2}$ cup oil. Sweeten with 1 tsp. sugar. Heat dressing
and add to salad while hot. The lettuce will wilt. Cool
the salad and dressing before serving. This is very tasty
indeed.

UNNAMED SALAD

1 medium head cabbage (shredded) $\frac{1}{2}$ tsp. celery seed
1$\frac{1}{2}$ cups cucumber (diced)   1/3 cup sugar
1 small onion (cut fine)   1 tbsp. Miracle
2 tbsp. vinegar   Whip dressing

Combine all vegetables, add vinegar, celery seed, sugar
and Miracle Whip dressing. Add salt and pepper to
taste. Mix well.

GERMAN POTATO SALAD

6 cups diced potatoes   2 tbsp. brown sugar
1 cup diced celery $\frac{1}{2}$ tsp. salt
$\frac{1}{2}$ cup dill pickles (diced) $\frac{1}{4}$ tsp. pepper
1 medium chopped onion   2 tbsp. vinegar
12 bacon slices   2 tbsp. water

Cook potatoes till tender, 10 minutes. Drain and dry.
Stir in celery, pickles and onions. Cover and keep warm.
Saute' bacon until crisp. Drain on paper towel. Crumble
and add to potato mixture. Keep some aside for garnish.
Pour bacon drippings in a cup. Return 2 tbsp. back
to frying pan. Stir in sugar, salt, pepper, vinegar and
water. Heat to boiling, stiring constantly, pour over
potato mixture. Toss lightly. Place in bowl. Garnish
with remaining bacon. Serve warm. Yeilds 6 servings.

SWEET TOMATO SAUCE

Peel tomatoes after scalding. Cut in small pieces and fill quart jars. Add 1 tbsp. sugar and 1 tsp. salt to each jar. Seal. Place jars in low boiling water and boil slowly for 45 minutes. Store. (Optional, sweeten with sugar if desired, when serving).

WHITE SAUCE

THIN:

1 tbsp. butter	1 cup milk
1 tbsp. flour	Sugar (optional)

MEDIUM:

1 tbsp. butter	1 cup milk
2 tbsp. flour	Sugar (optional)

THICK:

1 tbsp. butter	1 cup milk
3 tbsp. flour	Sugar (optional)

First melt butter in a skillet over high heat, (approx.) 2 minutes. Reduce heat and stir in flour, $\frac{1}{4}$ tsp. salt and pepper combined. Add milk while stirring constantly. Cook until smooth.

The stewing vat

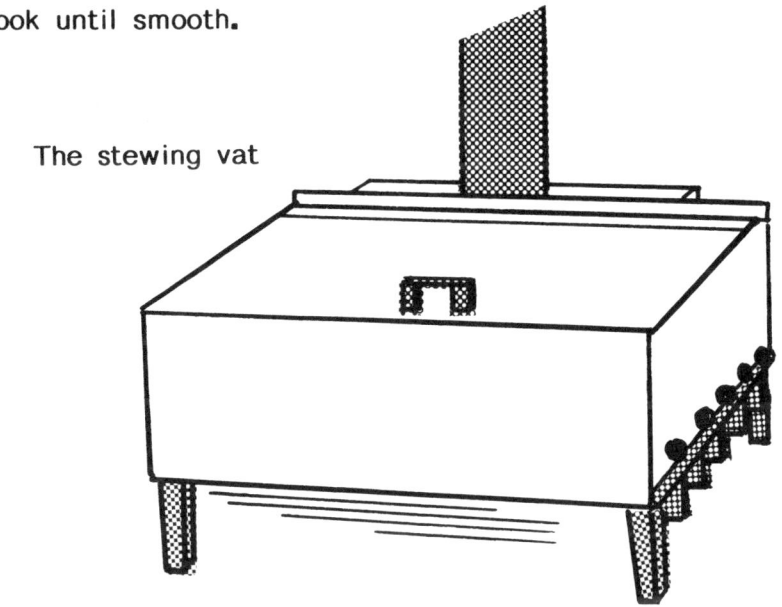

Main Dishes

CHICKEN PIE

5½ cups chicken meat
(chopped in small pieces)
5 cups bread crumbs
2 tbsp. onions
4½ cups milk

4 eggs

1½ tsp. salt
1/3 cup corn flake crumbs

Beat the eggs before combining with the other ingredients except the milk and corn flake crumbs. Place this mixture into a 10½" X 15" pan: spread evenly and pat down. Pour the milk over the pie. Finish off with sprinkling the corn flake crumbs on top. Bake at 400°F for 45 - 50 minutes.

CHICKEN LOAF

1 quart diced cooked chicken
2 cups bread crumbs
3/4 cup milk
1 tsp. sugar
2¼ tsp. salt

3/4 tsp. pepper
4 medium eggs
(separated)
¼ cup butter (melted)
1/3 cup chopped
pimentos

Soak bread crumbs in the milk for 5 minutes. Add salt, pepper, egg yolks, butter and pimentos. Beat the egg whites until stiff. Add to the chicken. Place in a buttered pan and bake for about 1 hour at 350°F.

ROASTED CABBAGE

4 cups cabbage (shredded)	3 tbsp. brown sugar
2 cups water	1tsp. salt
2 tbsp. lard	3 tbsp. flour

Here you will find a great difference in taste between fresh cabbage and soured cabbage. The sour cabbage has a unique taste of its own, try them both. Cook the cabbage in 2 cups water along with the salt stirring occasionally for 15-20 minutes, or until tender, add more water if necessary while cooking. Melt the lard in a sauce pan; combine the flour and cook til dark brown in color. Keep stirring steadily to avoid burning too much. It has to roast or burn slightly in order to brown, when the roasted lard is dark brown in color, sieve it into the cooked cabbage to remove all the burnt lumps.

Here you will have to decide how much roast you want in your cabbage. It is better to add less, than too much. Add the sugar while the cabbage is very hot. Serve hot only. Yields 2-3 servings.

FRIED POTATOES

Peel raw potatoes. Cut into halves or quarters. Cut each potato about the size of a large egg. Deep fry at 325°F till insides of fried potatoes are tender.

When oversalting food by mistake, drop a raw potato in it. It will absorb the excess salt.

To keep potatoes from sprouting, store apples with them.

THE BELL

On or beside every communal kitchen in the Hutterite colonies sits a large bell. This bell serves as a nerve cord to the Hutterite Community. It is a signalling device which not only alerts one that breakfast, dinner or supper is on the table, but it also lets one know the time of day or whatever is happening in the community. The length of time and the intensity that the bell is rung is interpreted by whoever the signal is given to. The various reasons the bell may ring are such as, for a meal to be served, work that requires members to come together, curfews for children, as well church services, etc.

Some modern colonies have replaced the bell with a siren. Each time the siren is used, a buzzer is activated in each apartment to alert people who may not hear the siren from the inside.

All in all, the bell or the siren serves its purpose quite well, and is yet another tool used in the colony to ensure participation and organization .

HUTTERITE HASH

3½ pounds ground meat
(duck, chicken, pork, beef
or what have you?)
2 eggs
3/4 cup bread crumbs

1 tbsp. salt
a dash of pepper
2 cups potatoes (ground)
¼ cup onions (minced)

Mix everything together in a baking dish and bake at 375°F for 30 minutes.

FRIED CHICKEN MIX

1¼ cup flour
¼ cup salt
1/8 cup accent
¼ tbsp. pepper
1/3 tbsp. oregano

¼ tbsp. garlic salt
¼ tbsp. thyme
¼ tbsp. cayenne
3/8 tbsp. cumin
¼ tbsp. paprika

Mix all ingredients together. Dip chicken pieces into egg and milk mixture, (1 large egg to 1 cup milk), then into seasoned flour. Deep fry in oil.

BAKED CHICKEN & SPAGHETTI
(1 serving)

3-4 pieces of chicken
1½ cup spaghetti noodles

1½ cup spaghetti sauce
1 cup mozzarella cheese
(sliced)

Bake chicken pieces at 400°F for 45 minutes, (wrapped in foil). Salt and pepper to taste. Drain juices from foil; brush chicken with spaghetti sauce and broil till dark brown. Let cool slightly and remove bones. Prepare spaghetti, place in casserole dish, add 1½ cup spaghetti sauce and chicken. Mix well. Add cayenne if desired. Top with mozzarella cheese slices. Bake at 375°F till cheese turns golden brown. Serve.

DEEP FRIED POTATOES

Peel raw potatoes. Slice the whole potato 1/8 inch thick. Rinse slices with cold water. Deep fry at 325°F till golden brown in color. Salt and pepper to taste. Fried potatoes for dinner are usually accompanied by shredded carrots.

BOBAK

1 cup butter
½ cup sugar
6 eggs
3 cups whole milk

6 cups flour
3 tbsp. baking powder
1 tsp salt

Mix all ingredients together. Place into a cake pan. Cut 2 inch pieces of homemade (or other) sausage. Mix about 8 pieces in each pan. That makes the Bobak very juicy. Bake at 325°F for ½ hour.

BACON CRISPIES

Cut the fat from smoked ham. Do not cut along any meat at all. Slice the fat 1/8 to ¼ inch wide. Heat a frying pan and fry the strips till golden brown in color, turning steadily to avoid burning. Drain on a paper towel. Serve with scrambled eggs and weekend buns. The Bacon Crispies are usually made for breakfast, every Sunday, all year round.

Food served in the colony conforms to a weekly pattern. This pattern also changes between the summer and winter seasons.

PORK PEROGIES

Filling:
1 cup ground pork
½ tsp. salt
dash of pepper
½ cup bread crumbs
¼ cup butter (melted)

Dough:
2 cups flour
1 egg (beaten)
3/4 cup water
½ tsp. salt

Cook the ground pork in 4 cups water for 5-10 minutes till all lumps are broken well. Drain thoroughly. Add ½ tsp. salt, pepper, bread crumbs and melted butter. Mix well. Mix salt with flour. Add egg, followed by the water and form a very soft dough. Dough should be a bit sticky to make hemming easier.

Roll the dough out in 4 inch diameter pieces, 1/8 inch thick. Place 1-2 tsp. of filling on each. Roll the ends up to the top and hem firmly.

Place in boiling water, boil slightly for 2 minutes. Perogies can also be deep fried until golden brown. When serving , pour fruit pudding over perogies. A meal of perogies in the Hutterite Colony is usually accompanied by buckwheat porridge.

HUTTERITE SPECIAL   (serves 5-7)

2 pounds beef or pork
(cooked and ground)
2½ cups chicken, duck
beef, or pork broth

3 large potatoes
(cooked and mashed)
4 cups corn
3 eggs

This recipe is usually prepared when enough left over beef or pork is available. It is a simple way to serve left over meat and potatoes. Combine and mix the beef or pork with the corn, broth and eggs, along with salt to taste, in a baking dish. Top with mashed potatoes. Bake at 450°F till top of potatoes is light brown.

SHMAGUS KNAEDLE
(potato fingers with cream gravy),

Grate potatoes first. Next, thoroughly squeeze out the water, using a cheese cloth or a new nylon stocking (panty hose). For this recipe you'll need 2 cups dry grated potato paste. Add:

2-3 tbsp. flour	1 tsp. salt

Combine and mix thoroughly to get a sticky paste. Using hands, press this paste into rolls, 2-3 inches long and 1 inch thick. Prepare the following:

1 tbsp. salt	2 tbsp. flour

Make a thin paste of this with ½ cup cold water. Add this paste to 2 quarts boiling water. This is necessary to keep the rolls from falling apart while boiling. Place the rolls into the boiling water and boil gently for 15-20 minutes. Drain water and smother with Shmagus. Shmagus recipe following this one. Serve with stewed chicken.

SHMAGUS
(Cream Gravy)

3½ cups whole milk	1 tbsp. sugar
½ cup melted margering	1 tsp. salt (or to taste)
3/4 cup flour	

Warm milk to luke warm. Add melted margerine and mix well. Combine flour, sugar and salt. Mix well. Add milk and margerine slowly, breaking lumps while adding. Using a double boiler, heat uncooked Shmagus to boiling point (till it starts bubbling). If Shmagus is too thick, add warm milk, and flour if too thin. (as desired). You may add Shmagus (cream gravy) to Knaedle, as well as baked or cooked potatoes.

POTATO DUMPLINGS

2 cups potatoes (grated) 2 tbsp. sour cream
1 cup flour 1 tsp. soda
1 egg

Squeeze the juice from the potatoes after grating, using a cheese cloth. Add flour, egg, sour cream, soda and salt. Mix well. Wet your hands and press the above mixture into small balls. Place in 2 quarts   boiling water, (add 1 tbsp. salt). Boil 20 minutes and drain. Prepare a white sauce, using 1 cup cream, 1 tsp. flour, salt to taste. Bring this mixture to a boil. Pour over dumplings.

HASH BROWN MIX CANDY

$2\frac{1}{2}$ cups water 2 potatoes, sliced 1/8 inch
1 1/3 cups flour thick, $\frac{1}{2}$ inch wide
1 tbsp. salt

Combine the flour and $\frac{1}{2}$ cup water and knead into a soft dough. Roll it out $\frac{1}{4}$ inch thick and cut in 1 inch wide strips. Bring 2 cups water to a boil in a saucepan. Add 1 tsp. salt and boil the strips of dough for 15 minutes. Drain the water from the dough strips and chill slightly to make cutting easier. Cut into small pea pod size pieces. Combine the dough with potato chips and mix well. Butter your griddle very heavily. If electric, set at 400°F. Fry the hash brown and mix candy until the potato chips are tender and have turned to a nice tan color. Keep turning steadily while frying. Yields 3-4 servings.

FRIED APPLES

Melt 2 tbsp. butter in skillet, add desired amount of sliced apples. Add sugar to taste and a pinch of cinnamon. Fry till light brown, turn over and fry other side. Serve warm.

FRIED NOODLES

Bring a small pan of water to a boil and place Hutterite noodles in the water. Boil slightly, if necessary, till noodles are tender. Thoroughly drain the noodles before frying in frying pan. Use butter for frying. Fry at 375°F till the noodles turn a light brown color.

SCALLOPED POTATOES
(small recipe)

2 tbsp. butter	3 cups sliced potatoes
1 tbsp. flour	1 tsp. salt
1 cup whole milk	$\frac{1}{4}$ cup onions (fine cut)

Melt butter in saucepan. Add flour, salt, milk and onions. Stir steadily till mixture boils and thickens. Add potatoes, keep stirring potatoes till it starts boiling again. Place in a greased casserole dish. Brush top heavily with butter. Bake at 350°F for 30-35 minutes.

In some colonies fried potatoes, noodles and stewed chicken are especially prepared for visitors from other colonies.

CHICKEN BURGERS

1 pound chicken meat (ground)	$\frac{1}{2}$ tsp. salt
2 cups bread crumbs	$\frac{1}{4}$ cup onions (minced)
2 eggs	1 3/4 cups milk

Combine all ingredients thoroughly, and fry and barbecue

any way you wish.

COTTAGE CHEESE PEROGIES

Filling:
2$\frac{1}{2}$ cups skim milk cottage
cheese
1/3 cup onions (minced)
1 large egg
1/3 cup bread crumbs

Dough:
1$\frac{1}{4}$ cup water
2 3/4 cup flour
1 tsp. salt

Fry the onions in margerine before combining with the

other ingredients. Beat the eggs before combining them

with the cottage cheese. Rub the cottage cheese with

your fingers to break it into small particles. Roll the

dough out 1/16 to 1/8 inch thick and cut 3/4 inches

in diameter. Place 1 heaping tbsp. of the filling on

each piece of dough and fold the sides up and hem

on the top. Fry in deep fat for 8-10 minutes or until

golden brown in color. Fry at 375 F. Serve with buckwheat

porridge and fruit pudding.

CLOBS. . . HUTTERITE DEEP FRIED HAMBURGERS

1 lb. hamburger meat (ground)	$\frac{1}{4}$ cup onion (minced)
1 tsp. salt	dash of pepper
1 cup potatoes (ground)	$\frac{1}{2}$ cup bread crumbs
1 egg	

Instead of beef, you can also use goose meat, or you

may use half beef and half goose meat. Beef is the

more popular of the two. Combine all the ingredients.

Add a small amount of water if necessary to make

the mixture a bit sticky to prevent the balls from

falling apart. Make balls the size of tennis balls and fry in deep fat, 15-20 minutes or until dark brown in color. The crisp, brown outside layer is about 1/8 inch thick. The inside is soft and tender. Fry at 375°F. Serve either hot or cold. Serve with cooked or baked potato, and cooked peas and carrots.

STEWED HAM STEAK

Use smoked ham for this recipe. Cut in 3/4 inch thick slices. Stew in half part lard and half part water. Add salt and pepper to taste. Stew until meat is tender. Serve with potato soup and Datchlen. Serve fruit moos for dessert.

CHICKEN STEAK

Cut steaks from breast of large broilers. Cut sideways, across the breast, 3/4 inches thick. Combine for seasoning:

$\frac{1}{2}$ cup salt   1 cup fine corn flake crumbs
$\frac{1}{4}$ cup tenderizer $1\frac{1}{2}$ cups flour
1 tbsp. black pepper

Rub steaks with seasoning thoroughly. Dip into milk and egg mixture. Sprinkle with seasoning. Fry each side of steaks in 1 inch deep fat for 10 minutes or until tender. Fry on low heat.

HACHINKA
(Baked Pork Side Ribs)

Chop enough side ribs for a meal into desired sizes. Ribs should have very little fat in it. Make seasoning with:

1 cup salt   1 tbsp. balck pepper
1 heaping tbsp. barbecue rub

Rub ribs thoroughly with seasoning. Place ribs into large pan, sprinkle with seasoning. Cover with foil. Bake

in oven at 400°F. till meat turns to a slightly brown color.
Reduce heat to 325°F and bake till tender.

WUCHDICH
(Steam Raised Dumplings)

Use an ordinary bread dough for this recipe. Add one
inch of Water to the bottom of a large kettle or use
a canning tub. Situate a rack about 4 inches above
hot water. Add 1 tbsp. lard to the water. Knead bread
dough after letting rise to double in size. Let rise again.
Form small balls about 2 inches in diameter. Let rise
once more. Place risen dough into rack in tub. Cover
tub. Bring water to a fast boil. Let boil vigorously for
7-10 minutes. Shut off heat. Let stand for 15 minutes
till steam settles. Pour a medium white sauce
over dumplings on your plate.

DATCHLEN
(Pastry Chips)

1¼ cups water   3 tbsp. shortening
2 3/4 cups flour   1 tsp. salt

Datchlen are usually made and eaten along with perogies and fruit pudding or buckwheat porridge. Make
a soft dough with above ingredients and roll out 1/8 -
¼ inch. Cut in squares or circles 3 inches in diameter.
Deep fry at 375°F till golden brown in color. Lay on
a paper towel to absorb excess fat. Serve. Use fruit
pudding as a dip for chips.

SLOPPY JOES

$2\frac{1}{2}$ lb. hamburger

1 medium onion (chopped)

$2\frac{1}{2}$ tbsp. worcestershire sauce

1/3 cup brown sugar

$\frac{1}{2}$ cup catsup

1 tbsp. mustard

2 tbsp. vinegar (optional)

1 10oz. can cream of
mushroom soup

Fry hamburger and onions along with salt and pepper to taste. Drain grease and add worchestershire sauce, sugar, catsup, mustard and mushroom soup. Heat and serve.

MAUL TASHEN

Dough:

1 egg

1 cup flour

$1\frac{1}{2}$ tsp. salt

1/3 cup water

Stuffing:

3 eggs (beaten)

2 tbsp. onions (minced)

$1\frac{1}{2}$ cup bread crumbs

$\frac{1}{4}$ cup melted butter

Roll the dough out in a 7 X 12 strip, 1/8 to $\frac{1}{4}$ inch thick. Spread the stuffing out over the other. Next, roll the strip up like a jelly roll. Hem the ends together. Place in 1 quart boiling water. Add 2 tsp. salt. Cook on medium heat for 20 minutes. Cut in small pieces before serving.

Baking

WHOLE WHEAT BREAD

2 pkgs. yeast
4 cups warm water
4 tsp. salt
¼ cup sugar
½ cup honey

½ cup chicken lard
8 cups unsifted whole wheat flour
4 cups white flour

Dissove yeast in 1 cup water and 1 tsp. sugar. Let foam lightly before adding to other ingredients. Mix all ingredients thoroughly. Add flour last of all. Knead into a soft dough. Let rise. Brush top with melted butter. Punch down and let rise again. Form into loaves and let rise. Bake at 350°F for approximately 1 hour.

WHOLE WHEAT BREAD

1 pkg. yeast
½ cup warm water
1 cup milk (scalded)
½ cup brown sugar

1 tbsp. salt
¼ cup melted lard
1 cup cool water
4 cups white flour
2 cups whole wheat flour

Dissolve yeast in warm water. Stir scalded milk with sugar, salt, and lard till melted. Add yeast and water. Slowly add flour and knead into a soft dough. Form 2 loaves. Bake at 350°F for approximately 55 minutes.

WHITE BREAD

2 pkgs. yeast
½ tbsp. sugar
1 cup warm water

¼ cup melted chicken lard
12-15 cups flour

3 3/4 cups milk (scalded)
2 tbsp. sugar

2 tbsp. salt

Dissolve yeast and ½ tbsp. sugar in water. Cool scalded milk to lukewarm, add all remaining ingredients; form a soft dough. Let rise till double in size. Punch down. Let rise again. Make loaves and bake at 350°F. till tops are brown.

WHITE BREAD

2 pkgs. yeast
2 tsp. sugar

½ cup warm water

Mix and let rise, then add the following:

2 cups milk (scalded)
2 cups cold water
4 tsp. salt

6 tbsp. haney
6 tbsp. lard (melted)
10 cups flour

Mix thoroughly. Add flour last. Knead into a soft dough. Let rise till double in size. Punch down. Form into loaves. Place in greased pans and let rise in a warm place for 1½ hours. Bake at 350°F for approximately 50 minutes. Makes 4 loaves.

WEEKEND BUNS

3½ cups milk	¼ cup chicken lard
1 tbsp. yeast	½ cup sugar and ¼ cup honey
1 tsp. honey	1 small egg
3 tbsp. butter	8 cups flour

Warm the milk to luke warm. Dissolve the yeast along with 1 tsp. honey in ½ cup milk. Yeast should foam lightly before adding to other ingredients. Melt the butter and lard: combine with milk, honey, sugar and egg, then mix well before adding flour. Knead into a soft dough. Let the dough rise 1 hour. Knead again. Next, let rise for 2 hours. Now you can form the buns. Form each bun in two parts, each part the size of a golf ball. Let rise before baking for 1 hour. Bake at 450°F. for 10-15 minutes or until the tops of the buns are light brown in color. Yields about 30 buns.

WEDDING BUNS

Instead of using ¼ cup of chicken lard as in the ordinary weekend buns, use ¼ cup of butter. Form the buns half the size of the weekend buns.

ZWIEBACK BUNS

1 cup milk (luke warm)	1 cup sugar
1 tsp. sugar	½ cup honey
1 pkg. yeast	2 tbsp. salt
3 cups scalded milk	1 tsp. baking powder
3/4 cup shortening	9 cups flour
2 eggs	

Dissolve yeast in 1 cup lukewarm milk and sugar. let foam lightly before adding other ingredients. Cream shortening, eggs, sugar

and honey together. Add salt and yeast mixture. Mix well.
Add flour, and baking powder. Knead into a soft dough.
Let rise in a warm place till double in size. Form dough
into walnut size balls, placing one ball on top of a
slightly larger ball. Let rise for 1 hour. Bake at 400°F
for 20-25 minutes. Brush tops with melted butter while
baking.

ROASTED ZWIEBACK

Using the zwieback Bun recipe, form large buns, about
4-5 inches in diameter. Let rise for 1 hour. Bake at
400°F for 30-35 minutes, till brown. Brush tops with meltec
butter while baking. Let cool. Cut in ½ inch thick slices.
Bake again at 250°F to 325°F till roasted dry to a golden
brown color. Store in a cool dry place.

When Hutterites were preparing for their voyage to
America, the women spent weeks making roasted
Zwieback and drying fruit to eat on the journey.

CORN BREAD

2 cups shortening
5½ tbsp. baking powder
2¼ cups brown sugar
5 cups milk

4 cups all-purpose flour
4 eggs (beaten)
4 cups cornmeal

Cream shortening: add brown sugar, milk and eggs. Add dry
ingredients, along with the yellow cornmeal. Mix slightly.

Pour into oiled pans and bake at 400°F for 25-30 minutes.

After bearing a child, a woman and her
family are given several small barrels of
ROASTED ZWIEBACK, baked especially
for her.

FRUIT POCKETS

Filling:

8 oz. package dried apricots	2 tbsp. flour
2 cups water	10 crackers (soda or
1½ cups sugar	graham)

Cook dried apricots in water until very soft. Add sugar
and flour. Cook 5 minutes: stir to prevent from
scorching. Remove from heat and beat with beater. Add
finely crushed crackers. Cool.

note; Dried peaches or any dried mixed fruit may be
used in place of apricots. May be made the day before.

Pastry:

1 pkg. yeast with 1 tsp. sugar	1 cup water (scalded)
½ cup lukewarm water	2 eggs (beaten)
3/4 cup sugar	½ cup butter (melted)
1 tbsp. salt	6 cups flour
1 cup milk (scalded)	

Dissolve yeast in ½ cup lukewarm water. Place sugar and
salt into a large bowl. Add scalded milk and water to
sugar and salt and stir until dissolved. Cool to lukewarm:
add yeast, eggs, and melted butter. Add 3 cups flour
gradually while beating till very smooth. Add enough
flour (3 cups), one at a time, to make a soft dough.
Turn onto floured board: Knead lightly. Place into a
greased bowl. Let rise in a warm place till double in size,
(about 1 hour). Punch down. Let rise again until almost
double in size, about 45 minutes.

Pockets:

Cut off small pieces and shape into 3½ inch diameter
pieces, thinner around the edges. Place a rounded tsp.
of filling per piece. Fold up the edge and seal firmly.
Place on a cookie sheet and let rise for 10-15 minutes.

Bake in oven at 350°F for 20 minutes until golden brown.

You may frost with the following: 2 tbsp. melted butter

with 3 tbsp. cream; add powdered sugar.

POPPY SEED BUNS

Cook:

1 cup poppy seed	2 cups cream

Cool above mixture and add:

2 eggs (beaten)	1 tbsp. cinnamon
1 cup sugar	2 cups raisins
flour to make a medium paste	1 tbsp. vanilla

Make a Dough:

2 tsp. yeast	$\frac{1}{2}$ cup milk lukewarm
1 tsp. sugar	

Mix and let rise. Add the following:

$1\frac{1}{2}$ cup milk (scalded)	$\frac{1}{2}$ tsp. salt
$\frac{1}{2}$ cup sugar	4 cups flour
2/3 cup margerine	

Make a soft dough. Let rise for 1 hour. Roll out thin;

cut in squares. Place 1-2 tbsp. of filling on each square.

Roll up and pinch ends together. Let rise $\frac{1}{2}$ hour. Bake

at 350°F for approximately 30 minutes.

MA'S RAISED PFEFFERNUSSE

1 cup lukewarm water	3 eggs
1 tbsp. yeast in 2 tsp. sugar	1 cup sugar
$\frac{1}{2}$ tsp. salt	$\frac{1}{4}$ tsp. cinnamon
2 cups scalded milk	flour to make dough
3/4 cup shortening	(7 cups or more)
3/4 cup molasses	a dash of pepper

Dissolve yeast in the water: let foam lightly before adding

to other ingredients. Combine milk, shortening and molasse

After letting mixture cool, add eggs. Mix flour and spices:

Add to above mixture and knead. Add more flour if dough

is too soft. Let rise. Cut small and roll with buttered han

Bake like buns at 375°F for 20 minutes, or till lightly browned. This recipe was most likely given to the Hutterische women from the Low German women when they lived across from each other by the Desna River in Russia.

SUGAR KUCHEN

Place ½ inch thick pie dough in round cake pan. Cover with 1/3 cup sugar (spread out), ¼ cup flour, ½ tsp. cinnamon and 1 tbsp. butter. Peel and cut 2 apples in slices and put on before topping. Top with 3 tbsp. heavy cream. Bake at 350°F for 45 minutes.

LEBKUCHEN

1¼ lb. granulated sugar   1 cup water

Boil above ingredients till it spins a thread. Remove syrup from heat and during constant stirring, add 1 pint honey. Cool to lukewarm. Mix together and add the following:

¼ cup butter   6 to 8 cups flour
1 to 1½ tsp. cardamon   1 tsp. soda
5 well-beaten egg yolks or
2 whole eggs

Be careful not to add too much flour - dough must be pliable enough to handle easily when rolling out.

Add ½ cup nuts - walnuts, almonds, or both. Chopped, candied peel may be added if desired. Mix dough, cover; let stand overnight. Roll out; cut with cookie cutter. Bake at 350°F for 10-12 minutes. Cookies should be only lightly browned. They must be stored in airtight containers for several weeks to ripen before they are really good. They should stay soft. This is a very old German recipe and is still a favourite Christmas cookie with many German peaple.

NEW YEARS KUCHEN

2 cups raisins
2¼ cup milk (lukewarm)
3/4 tbsp. dry yeast with ½ tsp. sugar
½ cup water (lukewarm)
½ cup sugar

1 tsp. salt
½ cup margerine
3 eggs
1 tsp. baking powder
8 cups flour

Soak raisins in hot water overnight. Drain before using. Dissolve yeast in ½ cup lukewarm water. Let foam before adding to other ingredients. Whip sugar, margerine, salt and eggs till fluffy. Add lukewarm milk, stir steadily. Add yeast. Stir and mix well. Add baking powder to flour, followed by raisins. Mix well. Add flour and raisins bit by bit to liquid mixture and knead into a soft dough. Let stan in a warm place for ½ hour. Knead down. Let rise for 1½ hours. Make balls the size of golf balls and deep fry at 300°F till dark brown.

JAM CAKE

1 cup cream
1 tsp. soda
1 cup sugar
1 tsp. cinnamon

3 eggs
½ cup jam
1½ cup flour

Dissolve soda in cream, add sugar and cinnamon. Mix well. Beat eggs together. Add to cream mixture. Add jam, beat till all lumps are gone. Last of all, add the flour, beat till smooth. Pour into cake pan. Bake at 350°F for 30-35 minutes.

RHUBARB KUCHEN

2 cups rhubarb
sugar to taste
1/3 cup cream

flour to thicken
2 tsp. cinnamon
or nutmeg

Cook diced rhubarb in water till tender. Drain water. Add cream. Add flour enough to thicken mixture. You may add sugar to your taste. Pour mixture into a pie shell. Sprinkle with cinnamon or nutmeg, whichever you prefer. Bake at 400°F for 20 minutes.

DOUGHNUTS WITH RAISINS

1 cup water with $\frac{1}{2}$ tsp. sugar
1 pkg. yeast
1 cup warm milk
1/3 cup sugar
2 eggs

1 cup raisins
$\frac{1}{2}$ tsp. baking powder
7 cups flour

Soak raisins overnight. Dissolve yeast in 1 cup lukewarm water with $\frac{1}{2}$ tsp. sugar. Let foam lightly before mixing with other ingredients. Combine and beat milk, sugar, and eggs till fluffy. Add yeast and mix well. Thoroughly mix raisins and baking powder with flour. Slowly add flour and raisins to liquid mixture and knead into a soft dough. Let rise for 1 hour in warm place till double in bulk. Roll out. Cut doughnuts and deep fry at 325°F till brown. Sprinkle with sugar while hot.

SALTY DOUGHNUTS

1 egg
$\frac{1}{2}$ cup milk (cool)
1/3 cup cream (cool)

$\frac{1}{2}$ tsp. baking powder
1 tsp. salt
4 cups flour

Combine egg, milk, cream, and salt together. Add flour and baking powder, knead into a stiff dough. Cut into doughnuts and deep fry at 325°F till brown. Sprinkle with salt while still hot. Good eaten with watermelon. Eat while fresh.

The Bread Box

RULL KUCHEN
(Doughnuts)

½ cup shortening
4 eggs
½ cup milk

1 tsp. salt
1 heaping tsp. baking powder
4½ cups flour

Combine ingredients, flour and baking powder last. Knead into a soft dough. Roll out ¼ inch thick and cut doughnuts. Deep fry at 325°F till light brown. Serve with watermelon or cantaloupe. Eat while fresh.

STRAWBERRY SHORTCAKE

3 eggs
1 cup sugar
1 tsp. vanilla
2 tsp. baking powder

1 cup sifted flour
½ tsp. salt
¼ cup cold water

Beat egg till thick and lemon coloured. Add sugar gradually. Beat till light and fluffy. Add water and vanilla. Add sifted dry ingredients. Blend till smooth. Pour into a greased 15 inch cake pan. Bake at 375°F for 12 minutes. Cut and serve with fresh strawberries and cream.

WHITE CAKE

2 1/8 cup flour
4 tbsp baking powder
1 tbsp salt
1½ cup sugar

½ cup shortening
1 cup milk
1 tbsp. vanilla
2/3 cup egg white

Sift flour, baking powder, salt and sugar together. Add wet ingredients except eggs and beat till smooth, (about 2 minutes). Add unbeaten egg whites and beat another 2 minutes. Bake at 350°F for 30 minutes.

HUTTERITE FRUIT CAKE

2 cups brown sugar   ½ tsp. salt
1 tsp. soda   2 eggs
1 tsp. nutmeg   1 tsp. cinnamon
1 cup buttermilk or sour milk
1 cup shortening
1 cup raisins or dried
apples or prunes or other
dried fruit
4 cups flour (more if coarse ground)
Nuts may be used if dredged with flour

Cream shortening, sugar and eggs. Beat. Add remaining ingredients: mix well to soften batter. Bake in two greased bread pans, 8 X 3 inches. Bake at 325°F for about 1½ hours or till a knife comes out clean when sticking it into the cake. If home-dried fruit is used, soak in warm water until soft. To store, wrap in foil and keep in a cool place. Yields 2 loaves of fruit cake.

PIE CRUST NO. 1

3 cups flour   1 cup melted lard
dash of salt   ice cold water

Mix flour, lard, and salt until fine. Add enough water to make a soft dough.

PIE CRUST NO. 2

1 cup shortening (melted)   3 cups flour
2 tbsp. vinegar   1/3 cup water
1 egg   1 tsp. salt

Mix flour, shortening and salt until fine. Add remaining ingredients and knead into a dough.

CREAM PIE

2½ cup milk
1¼ cup flour
1¼ cup sugar
4 eggs

2/3 cup butter
4 tsp. vanilla
2 10" pie shells
(#2 baked)

Heat milk. Mix flour and sugar together. Add to hot milk. Add eggs, butter and vanilla. Stirring steadily, cook till air bubbles start pushing to the top. Pour into baked pie shell. Top with whipped cream.

CUSTARD PIE

3 eggs
½ cup sugar
1/8 tsp. salt

2 cups scalede milk
1 tsp. vanilla
1/8 tsp. nutmeg

Beat eggs until light and foamy. Add the sugar, salt and blend well. add scalded milk and vianilla. Use Pie Crust No. 1 or No. 2. Brush with melted butter. Pour the custard into the pastry shell; sprinkle with nutmeg on top of the custard. Place rack on third glide from the bottom. Bake at 450°F for 10 minutes, then 325°F for approximately 25 minutes.

RHUBARB PIE

1 unbaked 9" pie shell
3 egg yolks (slightly beaten)
1 cup sugar
¼ tsp. salt

*¼ cup cream or milk
4 tbsp. flour
2 tbsp. melted butter
4 cups rhubarb

* If you use milk add 1 more tbsp. butter.

Mix all ingredients together and pour into pie shell. Bake for 45 minutes at 375°F. Beat egg whites, add 1/3 cup sugar and a pinch of Cream of Tartar. Spread on top. Sprinkle on coconut. Brown 8-10 minutes.

FRESH STRAWBERRY PIE

Boil until clear:

1 cup crushed berries   1 cup sugar
1 tbsp. cornstarch

Put fresh whole berries into bottom of baked pie shell.
Pour cooled filling over berries and chill. Serve with
whipped cream. Can also use mulberries.

TZUKKER PIE
(Sugar Pie)

2 cups cream   2 tsbp. flour
$\frac{1}{2}$ tsp. baking powder   1 tbsp. vanilla

Use Pie Crust No. 1. Add 1 cup sugar to 1 cup of above
mixture. Pour this mixture into empty pie shell. Spread
evenly, before baking, and sprinkle the top lightly with
cinnamon. Bake at 325°F for 20-25 or until brown. This
recipe will make 2 pies.

COTTAGE CHEESE PIE

$2\frac{1}{2}$ cups cottage cheese   3 tbsp. butter
1 cup cream   2 cups sugar
1 egg $\frac{1}{2}$cup flour
3 tbsp. corn syrup   1 tsp. salt

Use pie shell no. 2. Cream butter, sugar, and syrup. Add
eggs, keep stirring while adding flour and salt. Add cottag
cheese and cream last of all; mix well. Pour into pie
shell and bake at 350°F for 45-50 minutes or till a knife
inserted in center comes out clean.

To make it easier to cut
through a soft pie try a
buttered knife.

COTTAGE CHEESE PIE

2 cups skim milk dry
curds cottage cheese
1 cup sugar
¼ cup flour

2 eggs
1 tsp. salt
3/4 cream

Rub Cottage Cheese into small particles with fingers.
Mix with all other ingredients. Pour into pie shell no. 2
sprinkle with cinnamon. Bake at 350°F for approximately
55 miniutes.

PUMPKIN PIE

3 cups raw pumpkin
1½ cups sugar
½ cup molasses or syrup
4 eggs (beat yolks and whites separately)

1 tbsp. cinnamon
1 tbsp. ginger

Combine all ingredients except egg whites and mix well.
Add beaten egg whites last. Use Pie Crust No. 1. Spread
above mixture onto pie shell. Bake at 400°F until golden
brown or till knife inserted in the center comes out
clean.

SOFT MOLASSES COOKIES

½ cup lard
1 cup brown sugar
2 eggs
½ cup molasses
½ cup sour cream
1 tsp. vanilla
1 tsp. ginger

1 tsp. cinnamon
¼ tsp. cloves
4 cups flour
1 tsp. soda
½ tsp. baking powder
pinch of salt

Cream lard with brown sugar. Beat eggs before mixing with
lard and brown sugar. Add molasses. Mix flour with all
dry ingredients and add alternately to the cream mixture
with sour cream. Chill dough. Roll and bake on floured
baking sheet for 10 min. or till done, at 400°F.

STRITZEL NO. 1

Batter:

¼ cup butter	1 tsp. vanilla
3/4 cup sugar	¼ tsp. salt
1 egg	3 tsp. baking powder
2/3 cup milk	
1½ cups flour	

Stritzel Mix:

½ cup brown sugar	2 cups flour
2 tbsp. butter (room temp.)	1 tsp. cinnamon
	1 cup nutmeg (broken)

To make batter, first cream butter and sugar together. Add egg and beat well. Add milk and vanilla. Mix well. Mix dry ingredients together, mix well before adding to wet ingredients. Mix well. Prepare Stritzel mix by mixing all ingredients together. Pour half of Batter into a greased pan and sprinkle with half of stritzel mixture. Add remaining batter and top with other half of stritzel mix. Bake at 350°F for 30-35 minutes.

STRITZEL NO. 2

½ cup sugar	3 tbsp lard
2 tsp baking powder	2/3 cup milk
2 cups flour	

Mix and roll out like baking powder biscuits. Spread filling over;roll up and bake.

filling: (Mix in order)

1 cup sour cream	1 egg
½ cup jam	¼ tsp. baking soda
2 tbsp. molassas	1 tsp. baking powder
½ cup sugar	1/3 cup poppy seed

or:

1 small egg	½ cup sour cream
¼ cup brown sugar	¼ tsp. baking soda
1 tbsp. jam	½ tsp. baking powder
1 tbsp. molasses	1/3 cup poppy seed
1 tbsp. cocoa	

Add flour if mixture is too thin to roll up in pastry. Bake at 350°F till pastry is golden brown in color.

LIZZIE COOKIES

2 tbsp. shortening	$\frac{1}{2}$ tsp. lemon extract
1 cup sugar	$\frac{1}{2}$ tsp. soda
$\frac{1}{2}$ cup sour cream	$\frac{1}{2}$ tsp. baking powder
1 tbsp. molasses	flour

Cream shortening, sugar, sour cream and egg together. Add molasses, lemon extract and soda. Mix baking powder with 1 cup flour. Add to liquid mixture and beat. Add enough flour to enable you to roll out mixture. Roll out 1/8 inch thick, cut with round cookie cutter. Cut a hole in the center of half of the cookies. Bake at 350°F for 5-7 minutes. Place jam on the cookies with no hole, and place the ones with holes on top for a sandwich type cookie.

SHNECKI SQUARES

1 cup cream	$\frac{1}{2}$ tsp. salt
2 eggs	3 tsp. baking powder sifted
1 tbsp. sugar	with $1\frac{1}{2}$ cups flour

Mix in order given; add enough flour for a very soft dough. Roll out 3/4 inch thick. Cut into 4 inch squares. Bake 10-12 minutes at 375°F.

AGGAR DROP COOKIES

1 cup raisins	$\frac{1}{2}$ cup water
$\frac{1}{2}$ cup margarine	2 tsp. baking powder
1 large egg	1 tsp. vanilla
1 cup white sugar	1 tsp. salt
1 cup brown sugar	$2\frac{1}{4}$ cups flour
	2 tsp. cinnamon

Soak the raisins overnight. Beat the margarine, egg and sugar till creamy. Add vanilla and raisins, along with water and mix well. Combine all remaining dry ingredients before mixing thoroughly with wet ingredients.

Drop the batter onto a lightly greased cookie sheet, 1 tbsp. to each cookie. Place 3 inches apart. Bake at 350°F for 10 minutes.

HUTTERITE GINGER SNAPS

2/3 cup sugar
½ cup shortening
1 small egg
1/3 cup milk
4 tbsp. molasses
3 cups all-purpose flour

4 tbsp. Rogers Golden Syrup
1/8 tsp. cinnamon
1 tbsp. ginger
dash of pepper
1½ tsp. baking soda

Beat sugar, shortening and eggs till creamy. Add syrup, then milk, followed by molasses. Add spices and baking soda. Mix well. Next, add flour and knead into soft dough. Roll out 8 inch thick or less. Use a cookie cutter to cut out large ginger snaps. Bake at 375°F for 5-7 minutes. This recipe will make approximately 60 ginger snaps.

MARSHMALLOW GELATIN

2 tbsp. gelatin
½ cup cold water
2 cups sugar

3/4 cup water
½ tbsp. salt
2 tsp. vanilla

Soak gelatin in ½ cup cold water. Heat sugar in 3/4 cup water until dissolved. Combine gelatin mixture with dissolved sugar. Bring to a boil. Let cool to lukewarm. Add salt and vanilla. Beat until stiff. Use as glaze for next recipe.

Large numbers of WHITE COOKIES are baked at one time in many Hutterite colonies. Each family stores their share in airtight containers till consumed.

VANILLA WHITE COOKIES
(Christmas Cookies)

1 cup shortening
2 cups sugar
2 tbsp. vanilla
4 eggs (separated)
1 1/3 cups milk

4 cups flour
5 tsp. baking powder
1 tsp. salt

Cream shortening and sugar together, add vanilla. Beat egg yolk with above mixture followed by milk and salt. Thoroughly mix baking powder with flour. Add to liquid ingredients; mix well. Blend in egg whites. Drop onto a cookie sheet, 2-3 tbsp. to one cookie; spread out to 3-4". Bake at 350°F for 15 minutes. Glaze with Marshmallow Gelatin, (previous recipe).

WHOOPIE SANDWICH COOKIES

2 eggs
1 cup lard
1 tbsp. salt
3/4 cup cocoa
2 tsp. vanilla

2 cups sugar
5 cups flour
1 cup sour milk
1 cup hot water
2 tsp. soda

Mix eggs, lard and sugar in one container. Mix flour, salt and cocoa together in another and add alternately with sour milk. Last of all, add hot water and soda. Drop onto cookie sheet by spoonfuls. Bake at 375°F for 10-15 minutes.

Filling:

2 egg whites
2 tbsp. vanilla

¼ cup milk
4 cups powdered sugar

Beat the egg whites and add vanilla, milk and powdered sugar. Beat thoroughly. Add remaining powdered sugar and 1 cup Crisco; mix well. Place filling between 2 cookies.

SYRUP COOKIES

1 1/8 cups sour milk	2 tbsp. vanilla
1¼ tsp. soda	½ cup lard
3/4 cup brown sugar	1½ cups raisins
½ cup syrup	4 cups flour

Dissolve soda in milk. Add brown sugar, syrup and vanilla. Mix well. Add raisins to 4 cups flour. Add flour to liquid mixture bit by bit. Knead into a very soft dough, but not sticky. Roll out 1/8 to ¼ inch thick. Cut with a cookie cutter. Place on a cookie sheet and bake at 350°F for 20-25 minutes.

FLUFFY FROSTED COOKIES

Mix together 1 cup sugar and 1 cup sour cream. Sift together and add 3 cups flour, 3/4 tsp. soda, 1½ tsp. baking powder, ½ tsp. salt. Beat in 1 tsp. vanilla and 2 eggs. Roll out to ¼ inch thickness. If you prefer crisp cookies, roll thinner. For soft cookies, roll thicker. Cut into desired shapes. Bake until lightly browned at 375°F. When cool, frost with fluffy frosting.

FLUFFY FROSTING

Soak 2 envelopes gelatin in ¼ cup cold water. Bring 2 cups sugar and 1 cup hot water to a rapid boil. Add dissolved gelatin. Let cool slightly. Beat until stiff. Pile high on cookies and decorate with colored sugar, nuts, coconut or other decorettes. You can omit the frosting if you wish, and simply sprinkle the cookies with sugar.

ANGEL FOOD CAKE

whites of 11 large eggs
1 cup cake flour
1 cup white sugar

1 tsp. cream of tartar
1 tsp. vanilla
salt

Sift flour once; measure and sift six times. Measure and sift sugar the same way. Break eggs into galon size crock. Add a small pinch of salt. With wire beater, whisk to a froth. Add cream of tartar and continue beating until you can turn your crock over and the eggs will not slip out. Add vanilla. Fold in sugar bit by bit; then the flour the same way. Never stir: just lift and fold under. Bake slowly in an ungreased tube pan ½ hour at 275°F. Increase heat to 375°F and bake ½ hour longer. Turn upside down and let cool before removing from the pan.

TOPPING FOR CAKE

2 cups powdered sugar
1 heaping tbsp. shortening

¼ to 1/3 cup milk
¼ tsp. vanilla

RED DEVILS FOOD CAKE

Combine:

3/4 cup sugar

2 eggs well-beaten

Add:

1 cup thick sour cream

Sift:

1½ cups flour with 3 tbsp. cocoa

Add:

1 tsp. vanilla

¼ tsp. salt

Last, add 1 tsp. soda to ¼ cup hot water. Mix all ingredients well. Bake at 375°F for approximately 30 min.

BAKING TRADITIONS

Although traditions may vary between colonies, there are certain days in each colony when baking is done. On friday afternoon the weekend buns are baked. Some are carried to the homes, still piping hot, usually about 3:00, just in time for the afternoon coffee break. The bread is baked on mondays, while pies, cakes or or cookies are baked on thursdays mornings. At the 8:30 A.M. coffee break the first batch is usually ready and fresh baking is enjoyed by everybody.

Some colonies will bake gingersnaps twice a year, in both spring and fall. A large number are baked each time, many of which are stored in barrels or air tight containers and consumed day by day.

After the communal baking is done, some families will use the large oven while it is still very hot for roasting sunflower seeds, bake apples, apple chips, individual pies or cakes, etc.

During the winter months, when less baking is done, some colonies don't bake pies, cakes or cookies regularly each week. It is mostly during the busy summer months, when everybody is working very hard when most of the baking takes place.

Like in the rest of community activities, baking is always well planned in advance and organized amonst the female members of the colony, ensuring that good baking is available at all times.

The dough mixer

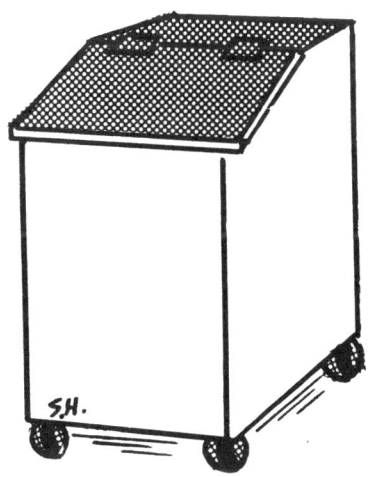

The portable flour box

Pickling & Canning

WATERMELON PICKLES

Peel watermelon. Cut into chunks. Sprinkle with pickling salt and let set for 2 hours. Pack into quart jars with dill and garlic. Use juice that has drained off; add water (if needed) to make 4 cups. Add 1 cup sugar and 1 cup vinegar; mix well. Pour on watermelon. Seel. Place into tub; fill with water to cover jars. Bring water ro a boil and turn off heat.

SOUR KRAUT

Cut cabbage fine, and pack loosely into quart jars. Add
2 tsp. pickling salt to each jar. Pour boiling water
over cabbage (slowly) and close tightly. Be sure your jars
and lids are clean.

SOUR KRAUT

Remove outside leaves before cutting cabbage (fine). Pack
tightly into crock, adding 1 cup pickling salt to every
7 quarts cabbage. Mix thoroughly. Pour enough water into
crock to cover cabbage. Set in a cool place to ferment
for at least 14 days. Place a heavy lid over
crock to keep cabbage pushed down. Scoop off foam every
other day. Pack loosely into quart jars and close tightly.

SAUER GEETSCH
(whole pickled watermelon)

Use small or medium sized watermelon. Make a brine of 3 gallons water, 1 cup pickling salt, ½ cup vinegar. Put dill in bottom of crock. Put in watermelon, another layer of dill until crock is as full as you want it. May add horse-radish leaves along with the dill; also garlic or chili peppers if wanted. Pour on brine to cover. Weigh down with board and clean rock. Skim off scum everyday. Ready in 3-4 weeks.

GARLIC SANDWICH PICKLES

3 quarts water (use ½ gallon jars, recipe makes 5 jars)

5 cups sugar
5 cups vinegar

Cook this brine for 2 to 5 minutes. Fill ½ gallon jars 3/4 full with sliced cucumbers. Place one clove of garlic on bottom, one in the middle and another on top. Place 1 tsp. salt and 1 head dill weed and a dash of pickling spice on top in each jar. Fill jars with hot brine. Seal and cook for 5 minutes.

GUETHEIT PICKLES

2 gallons sliced cucumbers
8 medium sliced onions
2 red peppers
2 green peppers
6 cloves garlic
12½ cups sugar

2 tsp. celery seed
7½ cups vinegar
2½ tsp. tumeric

Soak cucumbers in salted ice cold water for 3 hours. Use 3/4 cup salt for the recipe given. Drain. Pour vinegar, sugar and spices on pickles and heat to boiling point. Do not boil. Fill jars and seal it once. Set jars upside down. This recipe will give you 9 quarts.

SOUR PICKLES

8 quarts water
1¼ cups salt
5 cups vinegar

1 oz. pickling spice
1½ tsp. alum

Boil the water, salt and spices for 5 minutes. Shut off heat and add vinegar. Using gallon jars, put in clove garlic on the bottom, middle and top of jar. Place 1 head dill on top and place seal jars in water and cook for 2-5 minutes, just enough to let jars seal properly.

PICKLED EGGS

2 dozen hard boiled eggs
3 cups vinegar
1 cup water

1 tsp. salt
2 tsp. pickling spice

Peel the eggs and place in large jars. Boil all the ingredients in a pot for about 5 minutes. Pour this mixture over the egg. Seal jars and refridgerate. Pickled eggs can be eaten after 3 days, but not sooner.

SPECIAL TOMATO JUICE

12½ gallon tomato juice
2 quarts cooked blended celery
6 quarts parsley
6 quarts carrots, cooked and blended
2½ cooked green peppers (optional)

1 med. onion, cooked and blended (optional)
1 quart cooked and blended beets
2 cups sugar
1 cup salt

Mix all ingredients together except parsley. While boiling all the ingredients place parsley in a wire net and boil with other ingredients. Remove after 15 minutes. Boil the whole mixture for 30 minutes and pour into jars and seal while hot.

FREEZER PICKLES
(for 5 gallons)

5 gallons sliced cucumbers
1½ cups pickling salt
9 large onions (sliced)

5 cups vinegar
15 cups sugar

Prepare cucumbers; then, add pickling salt and onions. Mix well and refridgerate in covered container for 24 hours. Drain. Add sugar and vinegar. Mix well. Refridgerate another 24 hours. Finally, pack into containers and freeze.

FREEZER CREAM CORN

4½ quarts water
2 cups sugar

4 tbsp. salt
13 quarts corn

First mix ingredients except corn and bring to a boil. Add corn and cook on moderate heat for 5-10 minutes. Stir while cooking. Pour into plastic bags or plastic pails. Let cool overnight and freeze.

CANNED VEGETABLE SOUP

3 gallons water
3½ tbsp. salt
1 qt. string beans
1¼ cups carrots (diced)
1½ small celery (cut small)

1¼ qts. corn
1 head small cabbage
(chopped)
1 red pepper (diced)
1 large green pepper (diced)
6 medium onions (chopped)

Cook string beans in salt water till soft. Add carrots and celery and cook another 10 minutes. Add the rest of the ingredients and cook till tender.Fill jars with stew and steam for a full 30 minutes.

BREAD AND BUTTER CUCUMBERS

For this recipe use fairly big cucumbers as you'll want to peel them to eat them. First, to get the right ingredients, boil 1¼ cups salt in 2 quarts water for 2 minutes. Shut heat off completely and add 1 cup vinegar. Fill each quart jar with cucumbers, half full.To each jar add 1 clove garlic and a small dill head. Next, fill each jar to the top with the hot brine and seal. leave the jars at room temperature till the cucumbers change to a yellowish color. Store.

CANNED CORN

Pack quart jars tightly with corn and add 1 tsp. salt. Fill jar with hot water. Cook for 4 hours on low heat.

CANNED STRING BEANS

Clean and put cut beans in quart jars. Add 1 tsp. salt and add water to top of jar. Can for 3 hours on low heat.

CHOKE CHERRY AND GOOSEBERRY JAM

(small recipe)

4 cups chokecherries   water to cover berries
2 cups gooseberries.

Place Chokecherries and gooseberries in pot, add enough water to cover fruit. Boil for 10 minutes on medium heat. Sieve the juices from the chokecherries and gooseberries. Using the juices only, add the same volume amount of sugar as you have juice. Boil hard for 10 minutes and add 1 bottle Certo. Boil 1 more minute. Pour into jars. Set upside down to seal.

Miscellaneous

FRUIT PUDDING

5 cups water
2 apricots
2 peaches
¼ cup raisins

1/3 cup prunes
1 cup sugar
7/8 cup flour

Cut the peaches and apricots in small pieces. Cook all the fruit in the water for 10 minutes or until tender. Combine and mix the flour and sugar with the cooked fruit and water. Cook for another 7-8 minutes, stirring steadily to avoid burning. Cool before serving. Serve either alone or pour over any kind of perogies. Yields 2 quarts.

BAKED APPLES

Core large apples. In each apple put a mixture of brown and white sugar. Bake, cool and serve with cream.

MOTHER'S RICE PUDDING

4 cups milk with ½ tsp. salt   3/4 cup raisins
3/4 cup cooked rice

Cook above ingredients while stirring frequently, till rice turns very soft. Add 1 egg, ½ cup sugar, or more if desired. Add 2 tbsp. cream. Sprinkle with nutmeg or cinnamon and stir in.

Perogies topped with fruit pudding

BAKED CUSTARD

3 eggs (beaten)
1 tsp. salt
¼ cup sugar

1¼ cups flour
2 cups scalded milk
½ tsp. vanilla

Combine eggs, salt and sugar. Add milk slowly, stirring constantly. Add vanilla. Pour into custard cups. Sprinkle with nutmeg, Place custard cups in pan of hot water and bake at 325°F for 30 minutes or until a knife inserted halfway between center and rim comes out clean.
Serves 4.

HOMEMADE CHEEZE WHIZ

1 lb. butter
3 cups milk
2 level tbsp. salt
½ tsp. garlic powder (optional)
2½ cups water

6 lbs. process cheese

Using a pot, dissolve butter. Add milk, salt, garlic powder and water; mix well. Add cheese. Place in a double boiler and bring to a boil. Stir well to ensure that all lumps are dissolved. Sieve liquid cheese right into jars. Place jars into hot water and boil slightly to seal.

FRIED CORN MEAL MUSH

3 cups yellow corn meal
2 quarts water

1 tsp. salt
½ cup white flour

Bring water to a boil. Sift together corn meal, white flour and salt. Slowly add dry ingredients to boiling water, stirring constantly to prevent lumps. When well blended, cover and cook slowly in a double boiler for 2 hours or in a heavy pan on slow heat for 1 hour. Pour into flat pans to mold. Cut in slices ¼" thick and fry on griddle or in skillet until golden brown on both sides. Delicious with hot maple syrup or apple butter.

SPUDNUTS

1 1/3 cup milk	$\frac{1}{2}$ cup sugar
2 eggs	$\frac{1}{2}$ tsp. salt
4 tbsp. margarine	4 cups all-purpose flour
$4\frac{1}{2}$ tbsp. baking powder	

Combine all ingredients except flour and mix thoroughly. Mix in the flour while beating steadily.Fry in deep fat at 350°F. till the spudnuts are light brown in color.For average size, scoop 1 tbsp. of the batter for each spudnut. (optional)Dredge lighty with icing sugar while eating.

CREAM PUFFS

$\frac{1}{2}$ cup butter	1 tbsp. lard
2 cups hot water	2 cups flour
	8 eggs

Dissolve butter and lard in hot water while still on stove. Mix in 2 cups flour. Remove from heat and add eggs, one by one. Stir well. Place on pan by spoonful and bake at 375°F. for 15-20 minutes.

CHERRY MOOS

Bring to boil:

1 qt. water	1 cup sugar

Add 2 cups pitted cherries.Cook untill soft.

Combine and add:

$\frac{1}{2}$ cup sweet cream	1 heaping tbsp. flour

Boil for approximately 5 minutes longer on medium heat. Keep stirring steadily. Chill and serve.

GOOSEBERRY MOOS

Bring to a boil:

1 cup water   1 cup sugar

Add:

½ cup raisins   2 cups gooseberries

Cook mixture to soften gooseberries; while boiling, mix the following:

½ cup cream   1 heaping tbsp. flour

Cook for another 3-5 minutes on medium heat, stirring constantly to avoid burning. Chill before serving.

FRUIT MOOS

1½ cups raisins   2½ cups prunes

Cook above fruit together till very soft. Drain water; mix the following:

1½ cups water   4 cups milk
3 cups (day old cream)   6 whole cloves
1 tsp. cinnamon
(more if desired)

Bring to a boil.

Add:

3/4 cup sugar   ½ cup flour
½ tsp. salt

Stir well and let come to a full boil, stirring steadily. Cool at once in cool water, stirring steadily. When cool, add cooked fruit. Serve.

You can use other fruits as well, such as apricots and peaches. Fruit pudding or moos is usually poured over perogies.

BOOPOLA MOOS

4 tbsp. flour
1 egg yolk(beaten)
2 cups milk

pinch of salt
1 tbsp. vanilla
2 meduim sized bananas
whipped cream

Make a paste with flour and milk. Add milk gradually to avoid making lumps. Cook over low heat untill thick. Add egg yolk, bit by bit, while stirring to avoid making lumps. Add salt and vanilla. Mix well. let mixture cool. When cool, cut in bananas. Pour into pie shell. Top with whipped cream.

AHLE DOUCHLA
(Russian Pancakes)

3 eggs (beaten)
1 tsp. salt
1 tbsp. oil

$1\frac{1}{2}$ cups flour
$2\frac{1}{4}$ cups milk

Thoroughly mix all ingredients. Grease skillet heavily. Heat to very hot temperature. (400°F) Pour 1/3 cup batter into skillet. Brown on both sides. Sprinkle sugar over pancakes and serve.

RUSSIAN PANCAKES

1 egg
1 cup flour

$\frac{1}{2}$ tsp. salt
1 cup milk

Beat egg until light. Measure and sift flour and salt together. Add to beaten egg. Add milk gradually and beat until batter is smooth. You should have a very thin batter. Pour some pancake batter into very hot, greased frying pan, 400°F, allowing it to run over the entire surface of the pan in a thin layer. When edges turn to golden brown, flip and fry on the other side. Serve with butter and syrup or jam or just sugar. Variation: Pour a small amount of brandy over pancakes.

EGG PANCAKES

4 eggs
½ cup cream milk

½ cup flour
½ tsp. salt

Mix above ingredients together. Fry both sides in butter.

EGG PUDDING

5 eggs
2 3/4 cups milk

1 tsp. salt
¼ cup sugar

Combine all ingredients and mix well. Bake in a lightly greased baking dish at 350°F till lightly browned. Serve hot. Yields 3-4 servings.

COUNTRY VANILLA ICE CREAM

4 eggs
2½ cups sugar
5 cups milk

4 cups heavy cream
4½ tsp. vanilla
½ tsp. salt

Add sugar gradually to beaten eggs. Continue to beat until mixture is very stiff. Add remaining ingredients and mix thoroughly. Pour into gallon freezer and freeze.

HOMEMADE ICE CREAM

7 cups milk
4 eggs
7 tsp. flour
2 cups sugar
a dash of salt

2 tsp. vanilla
3 cups heavy cream
(or 3½ cups thin cream)

Scald milk. Beat eggs, add flour, sugar and salt; mix together. Slowly add hot milk into egg mixture, while stirring constantly. Bring to a boil. Remove from heat and cool thoroughly. Add vanilla to cream, whip a little, but not so much as to make it stiff. Mix cream with milk and egg mixture. Pour into containers and freeze.

For smoother ice cream, strain milk and egg mixture after cooking; before adding to cream.

GRAPE WINE
(basic directions)

1 gallon grapes   3 gallons water

For each gallon of water used, add 5 lbs. sugar. Ferment for 1 week. Take off juices and sieve 3 or 4 times. Pour into large jugs and let age. In the early part of aging process, don't screw lids on tight. Air should be allowed to escape.

BEET WINE
(basic directions)

Wash and cut tops from 8 lbs. of beets. Do not peel. Boil until done, in 3 quarts water. Remove beets and let juice cool. Add another 3 quarts of water, 1 lb. raisins and 3 oranges, (sliced). Add 1 cake compressed yeast, and 6 lbs. sugar. Stir once a day for 9 days. Sieve wine 2-3 times before pouring into large jars or jugs. Don't tighten lids. Let age.

You can pickle the beets after cooking them.

CHOKE CHERRY WINE

Let choke cherries stand till they are overipe. Then mash, using a potatoe masher. To each gallon of fruit, add one gallon of boiling water. Allow to stand for one week. Strain through a cheese cloth, extracting as much of the juice as possible. To each gallon of juice add 2 gallons of syrup made by boiling three pounds of sugar in one gallon of water.

Float a yeast cake on a piece of toast on the surface and allow to stand for 3 weeks before bottling.

Syphon into bottles or jugs. Don't close the lids tightly, so that the air can escape. The wine will be ready for drinking in 3 months after bottling.

PEANUT BRITTLE AT ITS BEST

Mix 3/4 cups sugar, $\frac{1}{2}$ cup corn syrup, $\frac{1}{4}$ cup water and 1 cup raw peanuts. Cook for 12-15 minutes. When peanuts begin to pop, take off heat. Add 1 tsp. soda and while foaming, pour out on well greased platters. Let cool, break into pieces.

PANCAKE SYRUP

2 cups brown sugar	$1\frac{1}{2}$ cup water
1 cup white sugar	2 tbls. butter

Mix above ingredients. Bring to a boil, and let boil for 3 minutes.

APPLE CHIPS

Core large apples. Slice 1/8" to $\frac{1}{4}$" thick. Each slice should be sliced evenly so drying will be consistent. Place apple slices on ordinary paper. Place paper on rack in oven and bake at 250°F till crisp; about 2 - $2\frac{1}{2}$ hours.

Sausages & Miscellaneous

HAM   SAUSAGES

6 lbs witts (chopped)
4 oz. witts fast cure mixture

Dissolve above mixtures in one gallon of cold water .
Grind 120 lbs. pork very course, using a 3/4 " or 3/8"
plate.   Mix ground pork with dissolved mixture very
thoroughly. Fill casings. Leave in a cool place for
48 hours. Do not freeze.   Next, place sausages in a
vat or tub of cold water.   Start heating very slowly
to 160 degees F.   This should take about 1 3/4 -
2 hours. Keep the temperature at 160 degrees for 4
hours.   After 4 hours, stick a meat thermometer into
sausages.   When the meat is between 150 degrees -
155 degrees the sausages are ready.
Remove from water and hang in a cool place for 12
hours. To store, freeze sausages.

GRITZ WURST
(Buckwheat Sausage)

Cook

1 hog head with a little fat on it until tender, after it has been cleaned and cut in pieces. Remove meat from bones. Grind meat. Fry 2 large onions (chopped) in lard, until tender. Add enough broth from cooked meat to 1 lb. buckwheat to cover well. Cook this gritz-broth mixture until tender. Cool and add to ground head meat. Add $\frac{1}{2}$ tsp. pepper and salt to taste. Put in beef casings and tie ends with string. Place in water used to boil the hog head and bring to a boil.

MUSH OR HEAD CHEESE

Clean the head of a hog well, remove brains, ears, and jaw bones. Cut into pieces: boil for about 2 hours or until tender. Boil the tongue, tail, heart, knee knuckles, and strips of skin from the cleaned hog with the head meat. The skins are very necessary for this dish because of the gelatine content. Care must be taken as the skins scorch easily on bottom of the kettle. It is thick but will form a little fat which rises to the top. Cook until this fat is clear, no longer cloudy. Cool and chop meat with fine blade of meat chopper and then heat meat in a heavy container.Stir constantly to prevent scorching. Season with pepper and salt to taste. About $\frac{1}{4}$ to $\frac{1}{2}$ cup salt. Remove from fire, pour into pudding pans to store in cold place. To serve, slice and place in oven until hot. Serve immediately on bread as a hot sandwich. Yields 2 - 4 gallons.

LIVER WURST

Thoroughly clean 1 hog head and cook until tender. Leave some skin and fat on it. After cooking, remove meat from bones and grind. Simmer one hog liver till barely done. Don't over cook it so it gets dry. Grind liver and add to ground head meat. Fry 2 large chopped onions in lard, till tender. Combine with meat. Add pepper and salt to taste; about ¼ cup salt. Push into beef casings and close ends together. You can also pack sausage into small jars and seal. Place in hot water and bring to a boil. Remove and cool well.

PORK KIDNEY SAUSAGES

1 heart (ground)
1 kidney (ground)
½ liver (ground)
8 cups water
¼ cup salt

16 lbs. pork (ground)
(pork should have fat on it)
1 tsp. pepper

Combine all the ingredients. The sausage filling should be a bit slippery when pushing into the casings. When pushing into the casings, prick each sausage several times to let the air out. Freeze the sausages. Thaw out before frying. Deep fry in ½ lard and ½ water. Fry or simmer slowly.

GRIPEN MIT AHLEN
(Cracklings with Eggs)

Heat or fry slightly enough cracklings for your family. Add 1 egg per person, salt or pepper to taste. Scramble and cook till set. Eat hot. Can also be eaten with catsup.

GRIPEN FLAKE
(Crackling Bread)

1 cup milk
2 tsp. baking powder
2 cups flour, or enough to make a soft dough

* 1 cup cracklings
dash of salt

Mix and roll out to fit cookie sheet, cut slightly (but not completely through) as in serving squares. Bake at 350°F till light brown, about 30 minutes.

* CRACKLING is made from freshly ground fat from the buchered hog and is fried or rendered till golden brown and then used in this bread.

SALOMI #1
(for 24 lbs.)

16 lbs. beef or venison (ground)
8 lbs. pork (ground)
3/4 cup tenderquick
½ cup salt
8 tbsp. brown sugar
6 tbsp. black pepper

3 tsp. cardomon
3 tsp. garlic powder
2 tsp. cayenne
¼ cup peppercorns
3 cups water

Combine all ingredients. Mix thoroughly. Push into sausage casings. Let sit in casings for 24 hours. Smoke sausage for 2 hours (if you prefer the smoke flavor). Bake in oven at 180°F to 190°F for 6-8 hours, or till meat thermometer reaches 140°F. Place pans beneath Salomi to catch drippings. Turn once every hour.

SALOMI #2
(for 50 lbs.)

35 lbs. beef or venison	$\frac{1}{4}$ cup cardomon
15 lbs. pork	$\frac{1}{4}$ cup all spice
3 cups tenderquick	$\frac{1}{4}$ cup garlic powder
2 cups brown sugar (packed)	8 tsp. cayenne
2 cups salt	1 cup peppercorns
2 cups black pepper	3/4 gallon water

Combine all ingredients. Mix thoroughly. Let sit in casings for 24 hours. Smoke sausage 2 hours; if you prefer the smoke flavor. Bake in oven at 180°F to 190°F for 6-8 hours or till meat thermometer reaches 140°F. Place pans beneath salomi to catch drippings.

PICKLED SAUSAGES

Brine for sausage:

1 gallon hot water	1 tsp. pepper
1 cup brown sugar (not packed)	
$\frac{1}{2}$ cup salt	1 tsp. saltpetre

Mix ingredients together to make brine. Pack sausages loosely into jars. Fill to top with brine. Boil for 1 hour on moderate heat.

Pork sausages hanging from rafters in the smoke house.

HUTTERITE PORK SAUSAGES

50 lbs. ground pork
3 oz. freeze and pickle spice
20 cups water
2 oz. pepper

$1\frac{1}{4}$ lbs. salt
$\frac{1}{2}$ cup sugar
sausage casings

To make sausages, first cool the pork almost to the point of freezing; at least till all the body heat is out. Grind the meat before mixing thoroughly with the other ingredients. First, mix and dissolve the dry ingredients in the water, lukewarm, then mix with the ground pork. Add more water if necessary. The mixture should be slightly slippery when pushing into the casings. When filling the casings, puncture holes along the sides to let the air escape. (About 8-10 holes per sausage). Hang the sausages at least 8 feet from the ground. When using 2" casings, let the sausages cool overnight, or smaller casings, the cooling will not take that long. You can let the temperature reach 30°F, but do not let it reach the freezing point. The next stop is to dry the sausages, using an electric or propane heater. Keep the temperature at 80-95°F for 4 hours. Do not let the temperature get above 100°F. That could result in souring and spoiling of the sausages.

The third step is the smoking. Using only hardwoods, smoke the sausages for 4 hours; keeping the temperature at 80-95°F.

In the last $1\frac{1}{2}$ hours of smoking set a pail of water on the coals and let it boil to create steam. This humidity will keep the meat from sticking to casings, thus, when removing the casings after cooking they can easily be peeled. After smoking let the sausages hang for another 12 hours before packing and freezing. Thaw and simmer the sausages before serving. Each Hutterite Colony butchers 12-24 big sows each fall, depending on the size of the colony. Alot of the meat is used for sausages. No sausages are made at all during the summer. It is always a pleasant change to start eating sausages in the late fall, along with winter food. Winter food consists largely of pork.

Extra Recipes

Index

HANDY CHARTS
TABLE OF KITCHEN MEASURES
(All Measurements Are Level)

A few grains	= less than 1/8 teaspoon
A dash	= 2 to 3 drops or a few grains
1 saltspoon	= $\frac{1}{4}$ teaspoon
1 tablespoon	= 3 teaspoons
1 cup	= 16 tablespoons
8 fluid ounces	= 1 cup
1 Imperial pint	= $2\frac{1}{2}$ cups
1 Imperial quart	= 5 cups
1 Imperial gallon	= 4 Imperial quarts

OVEN TEMPERATURE GUIDE

Description	°C	°F
Cool	110	225
Very slow	120	250
Slow	150	300
Moderately slow	170	340
Moderate	200	400
Moderately hot	220	425
Hot	230	475

SOLID MEASURES

STANDARD   METRIC

1 ounce .... 30 g
4 ounces (1/4 lb) .... 125 g
8 ounces (1/2 lb) .... 250 g
12 ounces (3/4 lb) .... 375 g
16 ounces (1 lb) . . . . 500 g
24 ounces (1 1/2 lbs) . . . . 750 g
32 ounces (2 lbs.) . . . . .1000 g (1kg)

FRACTIONS OF CUPS

7/8 cup = 14 tablespoons
3/4 cup = 12 tablespoons
2/3 cup = 10 2/3 tablespoons
1/8 cup = 2 tablespoons

1/2 cup = 8 tablespoons
1/3 cup = 5 1/3 tbls.
1/4 cup = 4 tablespoons

LIQUID MEASURES

IMPERIAL   METRIC

1 teaspoon . . . . 5 ml
1 tablespoon . . . . 20 ml
2 fluid ounces (1/2 cup) . . . . 62.5 ml
4 fluid ounces (1/2 cup) . . . . .125 ml
8 fluid ounces (1 cup) ....250 ml
1 pint (16 oz. - 2 c)* ....500 ml

* (The Imperial pint is equal to 20 fluid ounces.)

TABLE OF SUBSTITUTIONS

INGREDIENT	AMOUNT	SUBSTITUTE
Baking powder (phosphate or tartrate type)	1½ teaspoons	1 teaspoon double acting baking powder
	1 teaspoon	¼ teaspoon baking soda + 1 teaspoon cream of tartar
Butter	1 cup	1 cup margarine or 1 cup shortening or 7/8 cup lard plus ½ teaspoon salt
Chocolate	1 square unsweetened	3 tablespoons cocoa + 1 tablespoon butter or shortening
Cream	1 cup light cream	7/8 cup milk plus 3 tablespoons butter
	1 cup heavy cream	3/4 cup milk plus 1/3 cup butter
Eggs	1 whole egg	2 egg yolks
Flour (for thickener)	1 tablespoon	½ tablespoon cornstarch or 2 tsp. quick cooking tapioca
Flour	1 cup all-purpose	1 cup + 2 tablespoons cake flour
	1 cup cake flour	7/8 cup all-purpose flour
Meat stock	1 cup	1 bouillon cube dissolved in 1 cup hot water or 1 cup consomme
Milk	1 cup whole milk	1 cup skim plus 2 tablespoons butter or ½ cup evaporated milk + ½ cup water
	1 cup sour milk	1 tbsp. lemon juice or white vinegar + fresh whole milk to make 1 cup or 1 cup buttermilk

The Hutterite Treasury of Recipes as a GIFT ITEM!

Shipped anywhere in Canada and
the U.S.A. for **$10.00 each.**
To foreign countries add $1.00

order from:

HOFER PUBLISHING
(ON THE PRAIRIE)
719 McPHERSON AVE.
SASKATOON, SK.
S7N 0X9

Ship to: _____

□ Yes, I would like to order the **Hutterite Treasury of Recipes.**
□ Please ship_____copies. I'm
enclosing _____.

Name:_____
Address:_____City _____
Prov./State_____Code_____

□ Yes, I would like to order the **Hutterite Treasury of Recipes.**
□ Please ship_____copies. I'm
enclosing _____.

Name:_____
Address:_____City _____
Prov./State_____Code_____